VISHNU
An Introduction

To the gods
and to the demons
who dance in my dreams

Vishnu-Janardhana: deliverer of
mankind; North Indian stone carving

VISHNU
An Introduction

Devdutt Pattanaik

Vakils, Feffer and Simons Ltd.
Hague Building, 9, Sprott Road, Ballard Estate,
Mumbai 400 001

First printing 1998
Second printing 2000

Price Rs. 250/-

Published by Mrs. Jean Trindade
for Vakils, Feffer and Simons Ltd.
Hague Building, 9, Sprott Road, Ballard Estate
Mumbai 400 001. India

Printed by Arun K. Mehta at Vakil & Sons Ltd.
Industry Manor, Appasaheb Marathe Marg,
Worli, Mumbai 400 025. India

ISBN 81-87111-12-7

Contents

Acknowledgements

My parents, for enduring the pangs of my creativity

Mrs. Rama Balachandran, for her editorial insights and painstaking efforts to elevate the language of the book

Dr. Usha Bhatia, Guruji brothers, Mr. Kirit Mankodi and Mr. Rohit Pillai, for giving me access to their books and helping me compile illustrations

Minal, for helping me proof read the book

Giri and Shaila, for encouraging and enriching me

Mr. Arun Mehta, for believing in the project

The brilliant art-team at Vakil & Sons Ltd., especially Mr. Shrikant Mistry, Mr. Sudhakar Tawde, Mr. Satish Nagvekar, Mr. Jyotindra Saraiya and Mrs. Rajeshree Sabnis, for their enthusiasm and support in transforming this book into a reality

To Her, my *shakti*, may she always empower me

Thank You.

A Word About this Book

In the Hindu trinity of Brahma, Vishnu and Shiva, Vishnu is the protector of the cosmos who preserves life, making sure that all creatures enjoy a meaningful existence.

Respected by gods, feared by demons and adored by humans, Vishnu sits in the highest heaven Vaikuntha, instituting and maintaining the sacred, moral and ethical order of *dharma* to ensure harmony in the three worlds.

Whenever these laws are broken, whenever chaos and evil threaten the universe, Vishnu takes the form of man or beast to fight the forces of disorder and to reestablish *dharma*. Through these incarnations, or *avatars*, he maintains the integrity of the cosmic fabric.

Though Vishnu descended from Vaikuntha countless times, he is popularly known for his ten incarnations, the *dasha-avatar*. These are:

Matsya, the one-horned fish
Kurma, the mighty turtle
Varaha, the fierce boar
Narasimha, the man-lion
Vamana, the clever dwarf
Parashurama, the vengeful priest
Rama, the dutiful prince
Krishna, the righteous cowherd
Buddha, the compassionate sage
Kalki, the messiah

Several holy texts like *Shrimad Bhagavata Purana* mention many other incarnations, including:

Balaji, the cosmic child
Vishvarupa, the cosmic being
Yagna, the embodiment of sacrifice
Dharma, the personification of righteous laws
Dhanvantari, the celestial physician
Mohini, the enchantress
Hamsa, the wise swan
Hayagriva, the horse-headed warrior
Sanat-*kumars*, the four child-sages
Nara-Narayana, the twin practitioners of *tapas*
Dattatreya, the teacher of *Yoga* and *Tantra*
Narada, the champion of *bhakti*
Vyasa, the compiler of the *Vedas*
Kapila, the propounder of *Samkhya* philosophy
Rishabha, the *tirthankara*
Balarama, the lord of farmers
Prithu, the domesticator of earth
Mandhata, the establisher of *varna-ashrama dharma*

'Vishnu — an introduction' retells the tales of all these *avatar*s. It recounts the lores associated with Vishnu's consort, Lakshmi, goddess of wealth and fortune; his son, Madana, god of pleasure and joy; his companions and his devotees. It also reflects on the history and philosophy of Vishnu and the significance of many Vaishnava beliefs and practices.

Without support of myths, religious rituals and ceremonies lose their sacred meaning and become mechanical practices, open to mutilation and ridicule. Today, not many people know why Vishnu is sometimes represented by a *shalagrama* stone or why he is always worshipped with sprigs of the *tulsi* plant. Many hallowed practices that once provided psychological and spiritual support to the masses are gradually waning from the religious horizons of Indian society.

Myths and rituals are not merely products of faith. They are born out of man's need to explain his presence in the cosmos. They retain their validity in this modern world where the mystery of life still remains, despite advances in science. Sacred tales of gods and goddesses fill a void in our psyche and appeal to the core of our being, satisfying us in a way that logic and reason cannot.

For hundreds of years, tales of Vishnu have offered hope, love, strength and wisdom to the people of India. They were told and retold by bards in festivals and fairs.

This book brings together legends and lores from written and oral traditions of India to give an account of the heritage inspired by Vishnu. It does not claim to be an in-depth study of Vaishnava tales and traditions. It is, as the title states, an introduction. For those interested in a deeper knowledge of the subject, there is a bibliography at the end of the book.

I hope and pray that my book succeeds in animating the games gods play to amuse and uplift man.

And may it broaden the divine smile.

Devdutt Pattanaik

Makara-sankranti, 1999

Within infinite myths lies the Eternal Truth.
Who sees it all?
Varuna has but a thousand eyes,
Indra has a hundred,
And I, only two.

Vishnu as Venkatachalapati
(or Venkateshwara) who resides on
the Tirumala hill above Tirupati in
Andhra Pradesh

The Vaishnava Heritage

Chapter I

Vishnu in the *Veda*s

In the beginning, it was cold and dark.

Vishnu appeared on the horizon and filled the world with light. He took three steps — dawn, noon and dusk — and drove gloomy demons into the night.

With light came order, with order came life.

This is how the Vedic seers saw Vishnu: as a powerful life-bestowing, world-affirming sun-god who helped Indra and the *deva*s become masters of the universe.

Surya-Narayana: Vishnu, the sun-god; Kerala wood carving

Lord of *Yagna*

The *rishi*s felt the spirit of Vishnu reverberate in the *yagna* — the mystical ceremony that helped the sun rise, the rain fall and the gods wrest control of the three worlds. Hymns were chanted, rich oblations of milk and butter offered, as fires blazed brilliantly in sacred altars. Thus was Vishnu's power invoked and divine favour sought.

Vedic society evolved around the institution of *yagna*; priests lived to conduct it, kings sought to patronise it, and the common man was expected to work hard and pay for it.

It generated a rigid hierarchical caste-based society dominated by *brahmana*s and *kshatriya*s, where everyone was bound to his duty, his *dharma*. Vishnu, as lord of the sacrifice, was its foundation.

Vedic priests performing *yagna*; North Indian miniature painting

Fused image of Vishnu, Brahma, Shiva and Surya; North Indian stone carving

Cosmic Divinity

Not all were happy with these Vedic rituals; people toiled hard only to find their wealth being taken away by priests and kings who wished to please distant divinities. They sought a friendlier god, a god who solved their problems, shared his wealth and asked nothing in return. They found such a god in Nature — in the blue sky, in the black soil.

Some called him **Bhagavan**, the keeper of communal wealth, others called him **Narayana**, the deliverer of mankind. When he opened his eyes, day dawned; when he smiled, it rained. They saw him as a cowherd, a farmer, a warrior, a lover who freely offered everything he possessed. He was a single divine entity — the **Ekantika** — encompassing the whole cosmos within himself. He was **Vasudeva**, lord of the elements.

The *Pancharatra* sects extolled his virtues and invited all to adore, respect and worship him.

Vishnu and Bhagavatism

Around 500 B.C., the Buddha and the Jina moved away from rituals prescribed by the *Vedas* in favour of moral and ethical lifestyles.

Many turned towards Bhagavatism — the worship of Bhagavan: the god who did not demand sacrifice, who believed in *ahimsa* and *bhakti*. This cult, with priests and simple rituals of its own, became so popular that the orthodox were forced to look favourably upon the god of the people: **Bhagavan-Narayana-Vasudeva**.

In him they recognised the Vedic **Purusha** from whose body the whole cosmos, including human society, had been created. They identified him with **Vishnu**, lord of the all-powerful sacrifice, and welcomed him within the Vedic fold.

In *Narayaniya*, *Anugita* and *Harivamsa*, composed around 300 B.C., Narayana and Vishnu had become one. Their union led to the flowering of Vaishnavism, a powerful religious force based on non-violence, devotion and adoration of the divine. Vishnu became the sole manifestation of godhead, greater than *deva*s and *asura*s, not invoked by *yagna*s but pleased through *puja*s.

The mother-goddess Shree-Lakshmi, bestower of wealth and fortune, sought by both gods and demons, was seen as his chief consort, his *shakti*. Her presence made him more resplendent than ever. While he offered protection, she patronised growth. Together they became the divine foundation of human society.

Vishnu with his consort Lakshmi on Garuda, the eagle; South Indian bronze

2

Fusion through Vaishnavism

Devotees of Vishnu saw his spirit in great kings, sages and philosophers. They believed Vishnu manifested himself for the benefit of man.

The pantheon of *avatar*s evolved in the early centuries of the Christian era as Vishnu became increasingly identified with popular folk heroes (**Rama, Krishna**), legendary teachers (**Parashurama, Vyasa, Kapila**), ancient Vedic divinities (**Trivikrama, Akupara, Emusha**), tribal totems (lion, horse, eagle) and fertility gods (*naga*s). Early advocates of Bhagvatism, like **Narada, Nara, Narayana** and **Sanat-kumars** were also seen as *avatar*s of Vishnu. The concept of *avatar*s found the spirit of Vishnu in religious leaders like Sakyamuni **Buddha**, the Jain *tirthankara* **Rishabha**, the *tantrik* **Dattatreya**, bringing religious orders closer together and generating tolerance between different ways of life.

People could worship different gods believing that each one was an incarnation of one god — Vishnu. As a result, many cults and creeds merged with Vaishnavism.

Fusion with rival gods was not easy.

The middle ages saw the rise of Vaishnava and Shaiva rivalry: Shiva's favourite *bel* leaf was never offered to Vishnu while *tulsi* was kept out of Shaivite shrines.

Peace was restored when Vaishnavas recognised Vishnu in the wild Bhairava and Shaivas saw Shiva in the gentle Datta. The two gods merged to become **Hari-Hara**.

Hari-Hara: composite image of Vishnu (left-half) and Shiva (right-half) brought about by the essential unity of Vaishnava and Shaiva traditions; Mysore painting

Vishnu and World Religion

As hordes of invaders poured into India, destroying temples, crushing old ways of life, Vaishnavism helped adapt Hinduism to new ideas. Greeks found their hero Herakles in **Krishna**; the Zorastrian belief in the messiah

Kathakali performers from Kerala (left), folk dancers from Bengal (centre) and Manipuri dancers (right) bringing to stage the legends of Vishnu and his incarnations

3

Early Christian missionaries believed that the tale of Jesus Christ (top) inspired the legend of Krishna

Saoshyant was reflected in the prophecised descent of **Kalki**; the Puranic myth of **Matsya** saving Manu's ship appeared to be a variation of the Biblical tale of Noah's ark. Early Christian missionaries were convinced the legends of Krishna, the divine cowherd, were inspired by Christian gospels.

Vaishnavism also travelled to South-East Asia — *Suvarnadvipa* and *Suvarnabhumi* — where everyone adored the indigo coloured warrior-god Vishnu who rode on the great solar-bird Garuda and brought rain. The Thai kings of Siam declared that their capital Ayuthya was in fact the real Ayodhya, and that they were the descendants of Rama himself.

King of the Cosmos

In India, Vishnu temples became repositories of wealth and centres of political power. Under the eye of the benign god-king Vishnu, the arts flourished and kingship secured divine sanction.

Every ruler saw himself as the lord's *avatar*, born to uphold *dharma* within his tiny realm. Vishnu's resplendent *chakra* became the symbol of royal authority. A child born with this mark on his body, the oracles said, was destined to be king. The Gupta and Chalukyan emperors of India called themselves *chakravartins* — bearers of the universal disc — and tried to recreate Vaikuntha in their courts.

Idol of Vishnu riding Garuda from Thailand indicating the spread of the Vaishnava cult to South-East Asia

Focus of Philosophy

Assimilating political ideas, philosophical concepts and folk beliefs, Vaishnavism became popular amongst commoners and elite alike.

In Vishnu, *yogi*s saw the *purusha*, the soul of the cosmos; in his divine dreams, *tantrik*s found the powerful temptress *maya-shakti*, the substance of the world.

Vishnu was the fountainhead of *karma-yoga*, the doctrine of duty which was revered by every patriarch. His philosophical discourse, the *Bhagavad Gita*, gave solace to many troubled souls.

Vedantic scholars visualised life as the lord's game, *leela*, and the world as his playground, his *rangabhoomi*. Different schools of thought led by *acharya*s like Shankara, Ramanuja, Madhava and Vallabha were united in the belief that Vishnu was the supreme being.

Gateway of a Vishnu temple in South India

God of the People

Vaishnavism found a compromise between essential human equality and the traditional hierarchical world-view by emphasising more on devotion than on ritual.

Tales of Vishnu and the glory of his many *avatar*s reached every corner of the land through epics like the *Mahabharata* and the *Ramayana*. These were interpreted through song, dance, mime and drama, carved on rock, painted on cloth.

Vishnu as the noble Rama and the adorable Krishna fired the imagination of the masses. He was both dignified and delightful, a friend of the people capable of being whatever they wanted him to be: sage, warrior, lover, child.

Madhubani painting from Bihar inspired by the legend of Radha and Krishna (left); Shadow puppetry from Kerala based on the *Ramayana* (right)

Chaitanya, the Bengali mystic who considered Krishna to be his divine beloved

Tyagaraja, the Carnatic musician whose tunes were inspired by Rama

Power of *Bhakti*

Adoration of Vishnu was an inspiration for the flowering of vernacular literature. The 12 Alvar saints of South India wrote four thousand Tamil hymns in the seventh century A.D. in praise of the lord.

Around the thirteenth century, Ramananda took the cult of ecstatic devotion to the north. Soon the fertile plains of Ganga and Yamuna were reverberating with songs of Krishna's love for Radha, composed by Surdas and Meerabai. In Ayodhya and beyond, Tulsidas enthralled the people with legends of Rama's valour and nobility, rewritten in the language of the people, Hindi.

Jnaneshwar's Marathi translation of the *Gita* and Tukaram's devotional poems, the *abhanga*s, brought the word of the lord to the western corner of India. This was the period that saw Haridasa minstrels in the forests of Karnataka and Narsi Mehta in the villages of Gujarat. Everyone was singing songs about the blue god Krishna.

Around the same time, Shankardev took the lores of the *Bhagavata Purana* to Assam while Chaitanya danced in the streets of Bengal and Orissa enchanted by Krishna's charm. Eastern India echoed with the desire to unite with the divine.

Bhakti carved out routes across India, linking North and South, East and West, taking pilgrims to distant lands where Vishnu danced and sang. It united *Jambudvipa*, the rose-apple continent of India.

Today, Vishnu's religion is a major force in Hinduism. Its history has been one of tolerance and assimilation, of adapting old ideas to new ones. Whatever form it took through the ages, it never lost sight of the fact that embodied in Vishnu was the answer to life's mysteries, its divinity and its delight.

Tukaram, whose Marathi poems expressed his love for Vitthala

Vishnu Saves the World

Chapter II

The Hour of Doom

Before the beginning, there was an end: the end of the old era . . .

The world was decaying, degenerating, drifting towards destruction. Civilisation had crumbled, laws had collapsed. Cries of despair could be heard all around.

But Manu remained calm. "The lord will deliver us from this misery," he said confidently.

Nobody believed him. Nobody had faith.

Matsya, the Divine Fish

Manu was bathing in a river when a tiny fish called Matsya, swam into his hands. "Save me, Manu," he cried. "Save me from the big fish and I shall save the world."

Feeling sorry for the little creature, Manu carried him home in his water-pot.

The next day, Matsya had increased in size; the *kamandalu* could no longer hold him. He had to be put in a large urn. As the days passed, Matsya kept growing. Manu moved him from the urn to a well, from the well to a pond, then to a lake, and finally to the sea where he continued to grow.

"Who are you?" Manu asked the strange fish.

"I am **Vishnu**, the preserver of life," said Matsya revealing his divine nature.

Matsya: Vishnu's fish incarnation; South Indian bronze

Presence of Vishnu

Blue as the sky, dark as rain-clouds, draped in bright yellow robes, Vishnu was the personification of beauty.

Said the lord, "The world rests as the lotus in the palm of my hand, the cosmos revolves round my finger like a

Matsya, the divine fish, increasing his size to Manu's astonishment

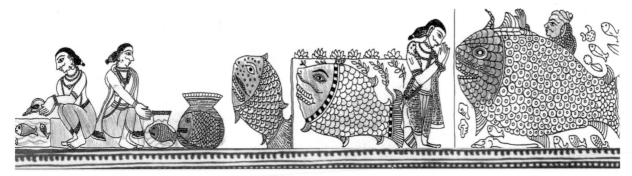

discus. I blow the music of life through my conch and wield my mace to protect all creatures."

In joy, Manu exclaimed, "You are **Janardhana**, the beloved benefactor of mankind. You exist, therefore existence is possible. You are eternal, therefore life is eternal."

Manu's Ship

Matsya revealed that in seven days, Shiva's arrow of destruction would herald the floods of doom to engulf the whole universe. "But the seed of life will survive if you do as you are told."

Instructed by Matsya, Manu gathered the seeds of all plants and a pair each of every bird and beast. He put them all in a huge ship and waited for the flood.

Vishnu bearing *sankha, chakra, gada* and *padma* — his conch, discus, mace and lotus; Modern calendar art

8

The Devastating Deluge

As foretold, after seven days, black clouds covered
the sun and hurled lightning in every direction.
Unrelenting rains lashed the ground. The seven rivers
began to swell and the four oceans started to
overflow. Waves as high as mountains drowned the earth.
This was *pralaya*, the final dissolution of
the cosmos.

On the horizon, Manu saw a great white horse with
red eyes, emerging from the sea. It was Badavagni
— the mare of destruction, a terrible beast that
breathed fire.

Riding it was a warrior dressed in black, soaked in blood.
With his flaming sword he cut down everything and
everyone in sight.

Kalki, the horseman of doom,
Vishnu's final *avatar* who heralds
the end of a world-cycle, *kalpa*;
Mysore painting

Kalki — The Saviour

"Who is he, my lord?" asked Manu.

"He is Kalki, the horseman of doom, sprung out of Shiva's
lethal dart," revealed Vishnu. "He is the saviour helping
the soul of man escape as he demolishes the imperfect
world. He too is me."

Wherever Kalki went, the waters of doom followed.

Manu was frightened. "Will *pralaya* consume this ship?
Will Kalki destroy me too?"

Vishnu smiled and said, "No, you are safe. Abandoning
ego, pride and desire, you placed yourself, without
reservation, in my protection. You will therefore survive
this catastrophe. When the new world reemerges, you will
be the first to live in it."

Matsya Recovers the *Veda*s

The divine fish Matsya sprouted a horn and harnessed
Manu's ship to it using Ananta-Sesha, the serpent
of Time, as the rope. He then towed the ship with its
precious cargo to safety, cutting through the agitated
waters.

Suddenly, Manu realised that he had, in his anxiety
to save life, forgotten to carry the books of knowledge —
the *Veda*s.

Matsya immediately plunged into the dark flood waters in
search of the sacred texts. He found them in the hands of
Damanaka, the demon of ignorance, who had taken
refuge in a conch-shell. Cracking Damanaka's skull with
his mace, the lord recovered the *Veda*s and gave them to
Manu for safekeeping.

9

Matsya killing Damanaka, the demon who stole the *Veda*s and hid in a conch-shell; Pahari painting

Cause of Cosmic Dissolution

Manu wondered why the world was being destroyed. "Are the gods angry with us?" he asked Matsya.

"Don't condemn the gods or the demons for the misdeeds of man," said the divine fish. "The cosmos survives on a set of laws called *dharma* that enables all creatures to live in harmony. Man has broken these sacred laws and unravelled the cosmic fabric beyond repair."

"Why did man abandon *dharma*?"

"Man was too obsessed with himself to think about the world."

These words of Matsya disturbed Manu. Man was responsible for his own downfall; no one else was to blame.

Atop Mount Meru

Matsya finally steered Manu's ship to Mount Meru, the eye of the apocalyptic storm. From its peak, Manu watched the earth being swallowed by the waves. "Is this the end?" he asked mournfully.

"The end? Nothing ends in the world; things only change. What you are witnessing is a destructive change of Nature: death before the rebirth." So saying, Matsya disappeared.

Wherever he looked, Manu could see nothing but the raging waters of *pralaya*. He was the lone survivor.

Manu bent his head and wept for the world that was.

Vishnu lying on the leaf that floats
on the waters of doom; South
Indian painting

Manu and other sages saluting Matsya who saved mankind from the flood of doom; Pahari painting

Cosmic Child

When Manu raised his head he saw floating on the ocean, tossed by the waves, a banyan leaf on which lay a dark child, suckling his right toe, unperturbed by the calamity that had befallen the world.

It was **Balaji**, the newborn cosmic child.

With a carefree smile Balaji negated the brutality of *pralaya*. His compassionate glance reassured Manu that life would go on.

Deliverer of Mankind

The divine infant took a deep breath and sucked Manu into his body.

Within, Manu saw the entire universe, all that had been consumed by the flood — the skies, the seas, the earth, gods, demons and humans, animals and plants — untainted by ugly thoughts and foul deeds.

Manu realised the child was none other than Vishnu who had withdrawn the world into himself. "You are truly **Narayana** — the deliverer of mankind," said Manu.

Chanting the blessed name of his saviour, "Narayana-Narayana," Manu became one with Vishnu, awaiting rebirth in the new world.

Vatapatrashayin: Vishnu on a banyan leaf; Tanjore painting

12

Vishnu Creates the Creator Chapter III

Vishnu's Slumber

After *pralaya*, there was a lull.

Nothing stirred. Vishnu rested in perfect tranquility on the endless coils of Ananta-Sesha, the serpent of Time, awaiting the reawakening of the world.

Around him, stretching into infinity, stood the still primeval waters. In them lay dissolved — without form or identity — all that once existed.

This was *yoga-nidra*, the cosmic slumber.

Birth of Brahma

Vishnu opened his eyes, setting the stage for creation.

The seed of life present in his body emerged from his navel as a thousand-petalled lotus. On it sat Brahma, the creator.

The creator looked in the four cardinal directions: he found nothing he could create the new world with.

He closed his eyes and pondered over the problem.

Padmanabha: Vishnu reclining over the cosmic waters on the endless coils of the serpent of Time with the lotus of life rising out of his navel on which sits Brahma, the creator; Pahari miniature painting

Vishvarupa: Vishnu's cosmic form
South Indian painting

Cosmic Being

"Mould the three worlds out of Vishnu's creative energy, his *maya*," a voice whispered in Brahma's ear. The creator opened his eyes to a splendid vision — the breathtaking cosmic form of Vishnu, his *vishvarupa*:

The lord's body encompassed the whole universe.

Within him was present the one cosmic soul; the two genders; the three strides of time; the four books of knowledge; the five elements; the six philosophies; the seven sheaths of the body; the eight directions; the nine emotions; the ten vital breaths; the twelve zodiacs; the fourteen planes of existence; the twenty-seven lunar asterisms; the thirty-three gods; the sixty-four arts; the seventy-two vocations; the hundred and eight divine spirits.

The celestial bodies made up his eyes; the oceans were contained in his stomach; the mountains were his bones;

the rivers flowed through his veins; the trees stood as his body-hair. His upper body was the sky; his lower body, the abyss.

From his right nostril he exhaled life, from the left he inhaled death.

He was the cosmic substance, *prakriti*, that gives form to existence; he was also the cosmic spirit, *purusha*, that gives life meaning.

He was infinite Space and eternal Time.

He was everything that was, is and will be.

He was the **Virat-purusha**, the entity that is the cosmos.

Sacrifice of Vishnu

Brahma said, "Without a sacrifice, *yagna*, nothing can be obtained. To create a new world, what shall I sacrifice?"

"Sacrifice me." said Vishnu.

"What shall I use as the sacrificial knife, the sacrificial altar and the sacrificial post?"

"Use me," said Vishnu.

"Where do I find the sacred fire and the sacred chants?"

"In me," said Vishnu.

"Who will be the presiding deity?"

"It will be me. I will also be the offering and the reward," said Vishnu.

Vishnu, the embodiment of every aspect of the cosmic sacrifice, became known as **Yagna-purusha**.

A Quarter of Vishnu

Brahma divided Vishnu into four parts. So vast was Vishnu, that from just one quarter of his being Brahma could create the whole world and everything in it, including the gods and the demons.

Vishnu was **Vastu-purusha**, the lord of Space, from which Brahma moulded the eight directions of the cosmic dwelling, its roof and its floor.

Vishnu was **Yuga-purusha**, the lord of Time, whom Brahma divided into the four ages — Krita, Treta, Dvapara, Kali — that make up one *kalpa*, the lifespan of a world.

Overwhelmed by the sheer magnificence of Vishnu, Brahma saluted him, "You are **Bhagavan**, the totality of the cosmos. Everything in this world has come from you."

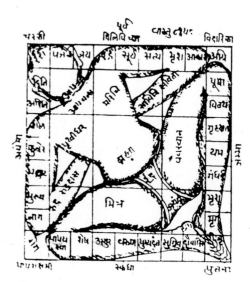

Vastu-purusha: Vishnu embodying the cosmic dwelling, its four cardinal directions, its four intermediate directions, its roof and floor

15

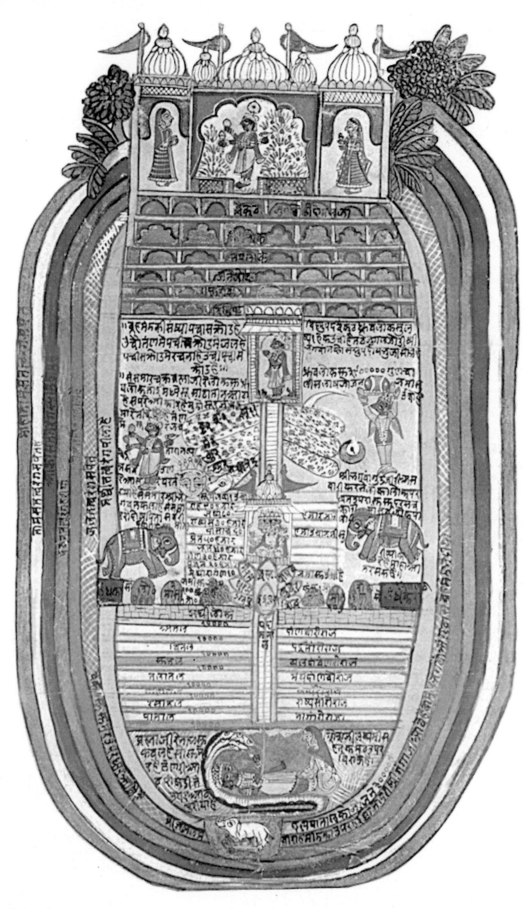

The multi-layered cosmos was
moulded out of Vishnu's divine
dream, his *maya*; Rajasthani
16   cloth painting

Churning of the Cosmic Ocean

First came the gods and the demons. As soon as they were created, they surveyed the cosmos — it was bereft of vitality.

"Where is everything?" they wondered.

Vishnu said, "All that you seek lies dissolved in the primeval waters. Churn it out."

"But what do we use as a churning spindle?" they asked.

"Use Mount Meru, the axis of Space."

"And for the churning rope?"

"Use Ananta-Sesha, the serpent of Time."

Emusha: Vishnu as the celestial boar who ploughed up the earth from beneath the cosmic waters; Temple carving

Emusha, the Divine Boar

Mount Meru lay submerged beneath the primeval waters. Neither the gods nor the demons could pull it out.

So Vishnu, took the form of **Emusha**, the celestial boar — his flanks stretched across the horizon, his snout reached into the heavens. Emusha plunged into the waters, ploughed up Meru with his mighty tusks and brought it to the surface.

Vishnu then wound Ananta-Sesha round the celestial mount to create the cosmic churn.

Kurma, the Divine Turtle

Turning into Kurma, a gigantic turtle, Vishnu supported the cosmic churn on his back.

So vast was Kurma that his upper shell made up the vault of the heavens and held the sky; his lower shell formed the abyss and contained the sea. His feet rested upon the four cardinal directions.

The gods and demons saluted this cosmic turtle. "You are **Akupara**, the celestial foundation of the universe."

Kurma's Strength

The gods held Sesha's tail, the demons grabbed his neck and they began churning the cosmic waters. But no matter how hard they strained, Mount Meru would not whirl. "Help us, Kurma," they cried, "Give us some of your abundant strength."

The divine turtle let his radiance invigorate the gods and the demons. Soon they were churning the ocean with ease.

The mountain twisted and turned, the ocean frothed and fumed. The new world would soon emerge.

Kurma: Vishnu as the divine turtle on whose back rests the entire cosmos; South Indian bronze

17

Shiva drinking the lethal poison, Kalakuta; Modern calendar print

Kalakuta — the Deadly Poison

After a thousand years of churning there rose from the ocean Kalakuta, the accumulated impurities of the old world. So terrible was this poison that it scorched Vishnu's skin, making him **Hari**, the tawny-one.

On Vishnu's request, Shiva collected the lethal fluid and drank it as if it was sweet wine.

The gods and demons began churning the waters — free of all impurities — with renewed vigour, convinced that success was close at hand.

Refreshing Rain

As the churning became intense, the rocks on the mountain slopes crashed into each other, spitting fire that set ablaze the trees atop Meru. Smoke filled the air — choking the gods and the demons. Eyes turned red, throats became dry.

"Help us, Kurma," they cried.

The divine turtle flapped its flippers and splashed water all around, putting out the fire, clearing the air, refreshing everyone.

Fabulous treasures emerging from the ocean churned by gods and demons; Pahari miniature painting

18

Rhythm of Life

As the churning continued, the formless, limitless mass within the cosmic waters began to take wonderful shape.

First came the sun, the moon and the pole star.

Vishnu placed the pole star above Mount Meru; the sun and moon danced round it. This gave rise to the cyclical rhythm of seasons, *ritu*. As spring turned to summer and summer to winter, plants began to flower and fruit while animals began to eat, mate, migrate and hibernate.

Vishnu, the pivot of this wheel of life, came to be known as **Chakrapani**.

Five Elements

Then came the elements — earth, fire, wind and water. + ether
But no sooner were they churned up than they began slipping away in different directions.

Vishnu stretched out his four hands and reined in the four escaping elements. Fire became his discus, water his lotus, wind his conch and earth his mace. He became ether and permeated every corner of space weaving all things into the cosmic fabric like the string in a necklace of beads.

With that, Vishnu came to be known as the lord of cohesion, **Vaikuntha**, he-who-prevents-disintegration.

Lakshmi and Her Gifts

As the churning continued, there emerged from the cosmic waters its most precious gift: Lakshmi, the goddess of fortune and splendour, bestower of power, prosperity and pleasure.

The goddess brought with her many gifts: Kamadhenu, the life-sustaining cow; Kalpavriksha, the wish-fulfilling tree; Kaustubha-Parasmani, the most radiant of jewels; Rambha, the celestial courtesan; Sura, the goddess of wine;

Sharangin: Vishnu bearing the celestial bow Sharanga which is the symbol of poise; South Indian bronze

19

Mohini serving nectar to the gods;
Modern painting

Airavata, the six-tusked, the white-skinned elephant;
Ucchaishrava, the seven-headed flying horse; Sharanga,
the perfect bow; and Panchajanya, the divine conch.

The Divine Physician

With Lakshmi came Dhanvantari, the divine physician.

Dhanvantari, the foe of disease, death and decay, contained
the spirit of Vishnu. He brought with him the science of
health and healing known as *Ayurveda*, a bag of herbs, a
leech to suck out toxins, a knife to cut out tumours, a pestle
and mortar to make medicinal pastes and potions.

In his jewelled hands he carried a pot of *amrita* — the
elixir of immortality.

Theft of *Amrita*

The demons grabbed the vessel from the hands of
Dhanvantari and ran away.

Angered by the theft, Vishnu decided to teach the demons
a lesson. He approached them taking the form of **Mohini**,
the enchantress, a voluptuous damsel with an alluring
smile and enticing eyes.

"May I serve the *amrita*?" asked Mohini.

"You may," said the demons, eager to please.

Mohini took the pot and began serving the nectar.

The demons, bewitched by her beauty, failed to notice
that she was pouring the divine drink only down the
throats of the gods.

Dhanvantari: Vishnu as the god of
medicine; North Indian stone carving

20

Rahu and Ketu

Rahu, suspicious of Mohini, sat amidst the gods disguised as one of them. The sun and the moon recognised the demon and alerted Vishnu. By then, however, some *amrita* had been poured into Rahu's mouth.

Vishnu immediately hurled his discus, the Sudarshan-*chakra*, and severed Rahu's neck preventing the nectar from entering his body.

Deprived of his body, Rahu swore to destroy his betrayers. He became the demon of eclipse that gnaws the bright faces of the sun and the moon from time to time.

His headless body became the astral entity known as Ketu.

Rahu enemy of the sun and the moon; Stone carving

Vishnu Defeats the *Asura*s

The demons realised Vishnu did not intend to give them even a drop of nectar. They were incensed, but it was too late. *Amrita* had transformed the gods into powerful, luminous *deva*s.

The demons, deprived of the drink, remained dark and gloomy *asura*s. Feeling betrayed, they attacked the gods.

Vishnu picked up Sharanga, the bow that had emerged from the cosmic sea, and shot deadly missiles at the *asura*s, helping the *deva*s push them into the deepest recesses of the cosmos, the *Patala*.

As the gods celebrated their victory, Vishnu blew the divine conch Panchajanya and placed the radiant jewel Kaustubha on his crown.

Lakshmi Marries Vishnu

Indra, eldest of the gods, invited Lakshmi to be his queen.

"No. Only Vishnu is worthy of me," said the goddess. "Did he not, as Matsya, save the seed of life? Did he not, as Kurma, help churn me out of the cosmic sea? He is canny enough to be Mohini, the enchantress, and trick the demons; capable enough, as the bowman **Sharangin**, to lead the gods. He will protect me, love and respect me."

Lakshmi placed the garland of victory, Vaijayanti, around Vishnu's neck and made him her beloved consort, **Vallabha**.

The gods cheered this union.

Brahma blessed it.

Lakshmi, goddess of affluence, beloved of Vishnu; Modern calendar print

Brahma riding Hamsa, the divine swan, a lesser known incarnation of Vishnu; Tanjore painting

Hamsa, the Divine Swan

Enchanted by the splendour of the three worlds, Brahma sprouted four heads and began admiring his creation from every angle.

"Contain your pride," said Vishnu. "The universe you have moulded out of my *maya* is not permanent. It exists today, but will be gone tomorrow."

"What is the purpose of such transitory existence?" asked the creator.

"*Samsara* exists to help man explore and experience the divine," replied Vishnu.

Vishnu then took the form of **Hamsa**, the swan, and began swimming in a river. The river did not restrain him in any way. He could fly away whenever he wished to, with not one drop of water burdening his wings.

Said Hamsa, "I enjoy the river; it helps me live. But I can fly only when I detach myself from the water. In the same way, he who seeks divinity must live in *samsara* without being attached to its flow."

Thus did Vishnu explain to Brahma the essence of life's mystery. The swan, the symbol of enlightenment and absolute freedom, became Brahma's mount.

Lakshmikanta: Vishnu, the beloved of goddess Shree-Lakshmi, bestower of power, prosperity and pleasure; Pahari painting

Vishnu Defeats the Demons

Chapter IV

Wrath of the Demons

After defeating the demons, the *deva*s, led by Indra, claimed every treasure that had emerged from the cosmic sea. Rising up to the heavens, *Swarga*, they became rulers of the cosmos. They warmed the earth, ushered in light and rain, made the tides rise, the moon wax and day dawn.

The *asura*s meanwhile sulked in *Patala*, the murky realm under the earth and sea. Angry and bitter, they took an oath, "We will oppose the gods in every way we can: what they generate, we will destroy. If they spread light, we will extend darkness. If they support life, we will stifle it."

They began attacking the gods — every day, every month, every year, every aeon, their victory causing winter to arrive, the tides to fall, the moon to wane and the sun to set.

The gods fought back.

The unending battles of *deva*s and *asura*s, the successes followed by failures, gave Nature its cyclical rhythm.

Madhu and Kaitabha

Two demons, Madhu and Kaitabha, decided to attack Brahma and arrest the creative process.

They climbed up the lotus stalk that emerged from Vishnu's navel and made their way to the seat of the creator. But Vishnu divined their intentioned. He grabbed them, placed them on his thighs, crushed them to death, and smeared their fat over earth, making it rich and fertile.

Vishnu leading Indra, king of the gods, towards the heavens after defeating the demons; North Indian painting

Vishnu riding into battle on Garuda, the celestial bird; Pahari painting

Madhusudana-Kaithabjit:
Vishnu defending Brahma from the
demons Madhu and Kaitabha;
Tantrik painting

Namuchi and Vritra

When Namuchi, the demon of darkness, locked away
light in his fortress, and Vritra, the demon of drought,
locked away moisture, the earth became dry, dark and
barren — plants withered, animals died.

Indra, king of the gods, tried subduing the two
demons but failed. "These demons can only be killed
by weapons that are neither solid nor liquid,"
disclosed Brahma.

Vishnu immediately collected the foam of the sea — that
is neither solid nor liquid — and fashioned out of it the
vajra, a weapon as powerful as a bolt of thunder.

Indra used this magnificent weapon first to kill
Namuchi and then Vritra. He razed their fortresses
to the ground, bringing light and moisture back into
the world.

Grateful for Vishnu's timely help, Indra called him
Upendra, his brother, friend and guide.

Death of Mura

Mura, the *asura*, had acquired the power to kill anyone
by his mere touch. So he stood before the gates of
Amravati, city of the gods, and challenged Indra to
a duel.

"I cannot fight him. If he touches me, I will die," said
Indra, trembling with fear.

"I will fight him then," said Vishnu, striding out to
face the demon. Looking straight into Mura's eyes,

I am never born
I never change
I am lord of all beings
Master of my own nature
By my own power I come to be

Whenever sacred law fails,
and evil raises its head
I descend:
To guard the righteous
To root out sinners
To establish sacred law
I am born from age to age

— Bhagavad Gita

24

Vishnu smiled and said, "Why are you so scared?
I won't bite."

"I am not scared," growled Mura, piqued by Vishnu's
words.

"Then why are you perspiring so much?" asked Vishnu.

"I am not perspiring at all."

"Yes, you are."

"No, I am not." So saying Mura rubbed his forehead
to prove there was not a drop of sweat on his
body. As soon as Mura touched himself, he choked
and died.

Hiranyakashipu's Immortality

Hiranyakashipu decided to get a boon that would make it
impossible for anyone, even Vishnu, to kill him.

He appeased Brahma who declared, "No man or beast can
kill Hiranyakashipu in daylight or in the dark, within or
without a house."

Secured by this boon, the demon-king launched an attack
on the heavens, defeated the gods and wrested control of
the cosmos, plunging it into darkness.

Narasimha Rescues Prahlada

Hiranyakashipu forbade the very mention of Vishnu's
name in his realm. But he could not stop his own son
Prahlada from chanting, "Narayana-Narayana."

Torture had no effect on Prahlada devotion.

Exasperated, Hiranyakashipu screeched, "Where can I
find Vishnu? I shall kill him and end your obsession once
and for all."

Prahlada said, "He is everywhere, even in the pillars of
your palace."

Hiranyakashipu smote a pillar. From within emerged a
magnificent monster that was neither man nor beast. It
was Vishnu in the form of Narasimha — the ferocious
man-lion!

Roaring lustily, Narasimha pounced upon
Hiranyakashipu, dragged him to the palace threshold,
that is neither inside a dwelling nor outside. There, at
twilight, which is neither day nor night, he ripped
open the demon's belly, pulled out his heart and drank
his blood.

Thus did Vishnu outwit the demon who tried outwitting
death.

Narasimha: Vishnu as the fierce
man-lion; Kerala wood carving

Narasimha killing Hiranyakashipu;
Calendar print

Vishnu Beheaded

The strength and guile of Vishnu made him famous
in the three worlds. The gods loved him, the sages
respected him, the demons admired him, though
grudgingly.

Once, the seven cosmic seers, the *sapta-rishi*s, keepers of
sacred wisdom, visited Amravati and found Vishnu
sitting beside Indra.

Saluting Vishnu, they said, "Without your support the
gods are powerless against the demons. You are greater
than the gods."

This comment of the sages upset the *deva*s. Jealous of
Vishnu's prowess and rising fame, they decided to
kill him.

They found Vishnu deep in thought resting his chin
on his bow. Turning into termites, they chewed the
taut bowstring until it snapped. The bowshaft
straightened with such force that it slashed Vishnu's
head off.

Vishnu resting his head on his bow
while the gods cut the bowstring

26

Horse-headed Vishnu

Without Vishnu, there was no one to stop the demons from stealing the sacred *Veda*s and mutilating its verses.

Saraswati, goddess of knowledge, cursed the gods who had harmed Vishnu. Ashamed of their conduct, consumed by guilt, the *deva*s decided to resurrect their benefactor.

They found Vishnu's body but not his head.

Vishnu's head had, unknown to them, become one with the sun, his long hair turning into rays of light.

"Find another head," said Indra.

The *deva*s placed the head of a horse on Vishnu's body and brought him back to life.

The horse-headed Vishnu, **Hayagriva**, defeated the demons and restored the *Veda*s to Saraswati who chose Vishnu as her eternal guardian.

Hayagriva: the horse-headed Vishnu, guardian of the *Veda*s; South Indian Bronze

Alms from Bali

Indra, proud of his many victories, once became so complacent that he refused to acknowledge the grace of Vishnu. Weakened by vanity, he was driven out of the heavens by the demon-king Bali.

Everyone loved, respected and obeyed Bali. In time, however, the adoration of his subjects and his absolute power inflated his ego. "I am lord of the three worlds. I can give anyone anything they want," he declared pompously.

"If you are so rich, can you give me three paces of land?" asked Vishnu, approaching Bali as **Vamana**, the dwarf.

"Is that all you want? Take it," said Bali.

Vamana Blinds Shukra

Something about Vamana made Shukra, *guru* of the *asura*s, very suspicious. "This dwarf could be sent by the gods. Don't give him anything," he warned Bali.

"What harm could this little one do?" argued Bali, picking up his *kamandalu* to pour water into Vamana's hand.

Once Bali poured water into Vamana's hand, Bali could not, by law, go back on his word. Knowing this, Shukra reduced himself in size, entered Bali's water-pot and blocked its snout with his head.

When water did not come out of the pot, Vamana divined Shukra's intentions. "There must be a choke in the snout," said Vamana to Bali, "Let me remove it."

Saraswati, goddess of knowledge, who accepted Vishnu as her guardian; Modern calendar print

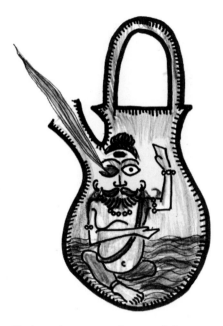

Shukra, the one-eyed *guru* of the demons

Vamana pushed a blade of grass into the water-pot and gouged out one of Shukra's eyes. The demon-priest leapt out of the *kamandalu* howling in agony.

Water then poured freely into Vamana's hand and he obtained from Bali full rights over all the land he could cover in three strides.

Two Steps of Vamana

In the blink of an eye, Vamana turned into the giant **Urugaya**. His legs stretched beyond the abyss and his head rose above the clouds.

With one step Vamana claimed the heavens — striding with ease across all the stars and planets of the astral realm.

The gods washed the lord's feet with the waters of Ganga, the celestial river, which was brought down to the world of man when Vamana took his second step to claim the earth.

Bali was overwhelmed by humility when he saw the lord's foot stretching across every horizon, overshadowing tall hills and vast plains.

Vamana, Vishnu's dwarf incarnation; Stone carving from Gujarat

28

Trivikrama: Vishnu-Vamana taking three steps to stride across three worlds;
Contemporary ivory carving from Kerala

Ganga, the river-goddess whose mount is a sea-monster, descended from the heavens clinging to Vamana's foot and became renowned as 'Vishnu-*padi*', she-who-sprang-from-the-foot-of-Vishnu; Mithila painting

Third Step of Vamana

"Where shall I place my third step?" asked Vamana.

Bowing his head, Bali said, "Place it on my pompous head that did not recognise Vishnu." Vamana shoved Bali back into the netherworld, where he belonged.

Vishnu's foot on Bali's head had crushed his ego, granted him salvation and transformed him into a divine demon.

Mankind mourned Bali: though a demon, his reign marked a period of peace and prosperity. For the benefit of mankind, Vishnu declared, "Once a year, after the rains, Bali shall rise from *Patala*. With him will rise the bounty of earth." This temporary ascent of Bali during harvest-time is a time of festivity and joy, celebrated as Onam in Kerala and as Diwali in the rest of India.

Vishnu, the God of Gods

Vishnu had done the impossible. He had conquered the cosmos — not by war, but by taking three steps! This conqueror of the three worlds, **Trivikrama**, was no ordinary god: he was god of gods, master of the universe — **Jagannatha**.

Gods, demons and humans saluted this great divinity.

Vaikuntha, the highest heaven, that stands above *Swarga*, became Vishnu's abode, whence he oversaw the welfare of the world, descending from time to time in various forms to battle forces that threatened harmony and order.

Jagannatha: Vishnu, guardian of the three worlds, preserver of life, standing between Brahma, the creator and Shiva, the destroyer; Modern calendar painting

Vishnu Establishes the Law

Chapter V

Varaha Saves Bhoodevi

The earth-goddess Bhoodevi floated on the sea, warmed by the sun, cooled by the rain. She always looked towards the sky, her back to the demons, and smiled at the gods.

Feeling slighted, Hiranyaksha, lord of the netherworld, dragged her down to his infernal kingdom under the sea and sought to make her his queen.

To rescue her, Vishnu turned into **Varaha**, a gigantic boar. Tail raised, hairs erect, he plunged into the sea and ripped through the waters until he reached the ocean floor where he found the earth-goddess in the clutches of the demon-king.

Varaha gored Hiranyaksha to death. Then with a triumphant snort, he placed Bhoodevi on his mighty tusks and carried her back to the surface of the sea.

Bhoodevi accepted Vishnu as her consort: trees and plants were their children.

Vishnu became the guardian of earth.

Bhoopati: Vishnu-Varaha, the guardian of the earth-goddess Bhoodevi; Comic book illustration

Vena's Ingratitude

Man and woman found food, clothing and shelter in the bountiful arms of Bhoodevi and expressed their gratitude through rituals, *yagna*s, *vrata*s and *puja*s.

But many saw no point in thanking the earth. "The earth is man's servant," said Vena under whose leadership mankind abandoned all rituals and began wrenching out the wealth of the earth-goddess.

Varaha fighting Hiranyaksha; Pahari painting

31

Varaha: Vishnu as the mighty boar raising the earth-goddess Bhoodevi from the ocean floor; North Indian stone carving

Death of Vena

Wise men decried this ingratitude. They begged Vena and his followers to change their ways.

"Beware the wrath of Vishnu," said the sages.

"What Vishnu? Who is he? Where is he? There is no Vishnu, there is no god. There is only man who worships himself with offerings of pleasure," said Vena.

Unable to tolerate Vena's callousness, the sages rose in revolt. They cursed and killed Vena.

Bhoodevi's Wrath

Despite Vena's death, the exploitation of earth continued.

Disgusted by the impudence of man and his insatiable greed Bhoodevi withheld her bounty: seeds did not sprout, plants did not grow, trees bore no flower or fruit. The earth became barren.

With no offerings or sacrifices, even the gods and the demons faced starvation. There was misery in the three worlds.

Purification of Vena's Body

Without food, there was despair and anarchy.

A leader was needed, someone who would make peace with Bhoodevi and restore order.

Everyone wondered where such a man could be found. "In Vena himself," informed the *sapta-rishi*s, the seven celestial seers.

The seers procured Vena's lifeless body and began rubbing its thigh vigorously till Vena's corrupt nature emerged from within in the form of a fierce demonic being that was driven into the darkness.

From the purified corpse the seers hoped to create the perfect king.

Birth of Prithu

From the arms of Vena's dead body, the *sapta-rishi*s drew out a strong and handsome youth called Prithu.

Celestial spirits, gods, demons, birds and beasts gathered around to witness this unique birth. In Prithu, they saw the spirit of Vishnu.

The celestial bow Sharanga fell from the heavens into Prithu's hand as soon as he was born, investing him with universal dominion.

Prithu Chases Bhoodevi

Prithu, the first consecrated king of mankind, found his subjects hungry and miserable.

Moved by their plight, Prithu begged Bhoodevi to have pity on them and give them food. She refused. Prithu threatened the earth-goddess with dire consequences if she did not release her wealth.

Bhoodevi did not give in. Instead, taking the form of a cow, she ran away.

Enraged by her defiance, Prithu mounted his chariot and followed Bhoodevi, pursuing her to the four corners of the world, determined to subjugate her.

Cowherd of the Cosmic Cow

Prithu raised his celestial bow to shoot a deadly missile at the stubborn earth-cow.

"I am the cosmic cow; my udders nourish life. If you kill me, you will destroy everything that exists," said Bhoodevi.

"I do not wish to kill you," explained Prithu. "I only want you to feed mankind."

"Why should I feed those who abuse me?"

"No one will abuse you ever again. I will make sure everyone treats you with respect," promised Prithu. "I will be your guardian, your cowherd, **Gopala**."

Sages draw Prithu out of Vena's corpse

34

Milking of the Earth

Prithu chasing the earth-cow; Pahari painting

Prithu taught mankind agriculture, cattle rearing, mining and trade. He instituted the principle of prudent economics, *artha*, that supports human society without harming Nature.

Under Prithu's watchful eye, the wealth of the earth was milked wisely by man, gods, demons, sages, *naga*s, *gandharva*s, *yaksha*s and every other celestial spirit.

In the earth-cow, mankind found sustenance, artists found inspiration, scholars found wisdom, priests found sacred chants, mystics found insights. The *deva*s procured energising potions, the *asura*s obtained intoxicating drinks. *Gandharva*s found music, *apsara*s found beauty, *vidyadhara*s found magic. Cattle got grass snakes got venom bees got honey.

Bhoodevi satisfied everyone's needs. She was worshipped and adored by all as Prithvi: the beloved of Prithu.

Bhoodevi's Fear

The three worlds thanked Vishnu for making peace with Bhoodevi.

But there was fear in the heart of the earth-goddess. "What if there is another Vena in the future?" she asked the lord.

35

The Bull of Dharma; seal from the Indus valley, 1500 B.C.

"Fear not," said Vishnu. "I will institute *dharma*: laws that will guarantee your well being. Whenever these laws are broken I will descend upon earth to punish the transgressor."

Bull of *Dharma*

From Vishnu's chest rose a bull. "Behold, the bull of *dharma*. Love, truth, discipline and compassion are its four limbs. So long as it stands upright, the world will survive," said the lord.

Brahma revealed, "Every time this bull of *dharma* loses a leg, an age will come to an end. The first age to come to an end will be the age of perfection, Krita-*yuga*. After this will come Treta and Dvapara *yugas*, periods of increasing corruption. Finally, when the bull stands on only one foot it will be the age of Kali, the age of materialism and spiritual blindness, at the end of which the floods of doom will engulf the earth."

Birth of Mandhata

In Krita-*yuga*, Vishnu descended upon earth as Mandhata, to teach mankind the ways of *dharma*.

Yuvanashva, king of the world, had many wives but no children. So the sages of earth gave him a pot of holy water, potent enough to give anyone a child. "Keep the pot under your bed for one night; at dawn let your favourite queen drink the water," said the sages.

The king kept the pot of water under his bed as he was told. But in the middle of the night, he woke up feeling thirsty and accidentally drank the sacred water.

As a result he became pregnant.

Serpents milking the earth-cow under Prithu's watchful eye; Pahari painting

36

Nine months later, Yuvanashva experienced the pangs of labour. The gods descended from the heavens to deliver the child. They cut open the king's side and pulled it out.

"How will I, a man, nurse this child?" wondered Yuvanashva.

"I will feed it," said Indra, king of the gods, placing his divine finger that oozed milk in the child's mouth.

This child, born of a man, nursed by a god, was Mandhata — the best of kings.

Gopala: keeper of the cosmic-cow; Modern calendar print

Duties of Man

Mandhata defined the duties of every member of society based on *dharma*: *brahmanas* looked after the spiritual and intellectual needs of society; *kshatriyas* took care of its defence and administration; *vaishyas* ensured its material welfare; *shudras* through service and skill, supported its very foundations. No group, *varna*, dominated the world.

Said Mandhata, "Without *dharma*, economics and politics is corrupt, pleasure is vulgar, and the quest for salvation, escapism."

During Mandhata's reign every man performed his duty. Mankind respected the laws of society and the cycles of Nature to live in harmony with the world around.

It was a golden age.

Mandhata's Penance

Mandhata's virtue inspired the people of earth to lead virtuous lives filled with love, truth, discipline and compassion. Man's virtue pleased the gods who sprinkled rain and made the earth fertile.

One year the rains did not come. Indra, lord of the celestial realm, told Mandhata, "Someone in your land is not respecting *dharma*. I will let the rains fall only if you kill the culprit."

Mandhata refused to kill anyone. He said, "If one of my subjects is breaking the sacred law, it means that I, as king, have failed in my duty."

Mandhata punished himself: he fasted, walked on fire, slept on ice. Watching Mandhata suffer for their sake, those who had broken the sacred laws mended their ways.

Indra let the rains fall on earth.

Stages of Life

Having completed his duties as king and householder, Mandhata decided to renounce the world. "As part of *samsara*, I have fulfilled all my obligations. I have made good use of wealth and power and have enjoyed all the pleasures of life. Now, it is time to go beyond these material things. I seek *moksha*."

"Why now?" asked his people.

"In the first part of my life, as a *brahmachari*, I prepared myself to live in this world; then I became a *grihasthi*, a householder and a responsible member of society. Now it is time to become a *vanaprasthi*, a forest-dweller, renounce the world to make way for the next generation. Only then can I become a *sanyasi*, free to liberate the spirit from the confines of the body, the limitations of the mind and the domination of the ego."

After crowning a worthy successor, Mandhata abandoned all contact with human society and returned whence he had come — to the heart of Vishnu.

Mandhata (centre) surrounded by (top row from left) a *brahmana, kshatriya, vaishya, shudra* and (bottom row from left) a *brahmachari, grihasti, vanaprasthi* and *sanyasi*

Vishnu Descends as Rama

Chapter VI

Reign of Terror

In the Krita-*yuga*, Mandhata bestowed upon *kshatriya*s the power to defend law and land.

But as time passed, corruption seeped into society. Kings and warriors, motivated by desire, not duty, began abusing their military might to oppress society and plunder its wealth.

Kartaviryarjuna, the king of Haihaiyas, acquired a thousand arms from Vishnu himself, ostensibly to protect the earth. But he used them to steal cows.

With that, the age of perfection came to an end and Treta-*yuga*, the less-than-ideal second quarter of the world-cycle, dawned.

Urva's Wrath

Kartaviryarjuna once raided the hermitage of the Bhargava *brahmana*s and stole their cows. Sage Chyavana, leader of the Bhargavas, tried to make peace but was killed by the Haihaiya king.

Chyavana's son Urva was still in his mother's womb when he learnt of his father's death. The rage of this unborn child took the form of a blazing fire that threatened to destroy the whole world.

Vishnu said to the vengeful infant, "Do not punish the whole world for the crime of one king."

Hearing Vishnu, Urva flung the flames of his fury into the sea where it turned into Badavagni, the mare of destruction. "It will remain under the sea till the end of Kali-*yuga* when the world becomes totally corrupt, beyond redemption," said Urva.

Birth of Bhargava-Rama

Vishnu promised to avenge Chyavana's death and punish every *kshatriya* who had strayed from the path of *dharma*.

He took birth in the Bhargava clan as Rama, the youngest son of sage Jamadagni and his wife Renuka.

Though born in a family of priests, Rama had the disposition of a warrior. He learnt the art of war from Shiva himself and became an expert in the use of the axe earning the title **Parashurama**, Rama-who-wields-the-axe.

Badavagni, the mare of doom, the mount of Kalki, the final *avatar* of Vishnu; Tribal metal art, Madhya Pradesh

Kamadhenu, the wish-fulfilling cow, a manifestation of the goddess Lakshmi

Death of Kartaviryarjuna

Jamadagni was the guardian of Kamadhenu, the celestial cow which provided enough milk to feed an army a day.

When Kartaviryarjuna learnt about this miraculous cow, he came to Jamadagni's hermitage and forcibly dragged Kamadhenu to his palace.

"If kings of the earth act like thieves, who will protect the weak?" asked Parashurama. Kartaviryarjuna did not reply. So the lord picked up his axe and hacked the greedy king to death.

Having soiled his hands with blood, Parashurama went on a pilgrimage to purify himself.

Parashurama's Vow

While Parashurama was away, Kartaviryarjuna's sons decided to avenge their father's death. They raided the Bhargava hermitage and beheaded Jamadagni.

As he watched his mother cry during his father's cremation, Parashurama took an oath, "Twenty one times did my mother beat her chest as she mourned for my father; twenty one times shall I make the *kshatriya*-women of the world weep for their husbands."

He swore to kill every warrior and king on the face of the earth who had subverted the law of the land for personal gain.

Massacre of Warriors

Parashurama fulfilled his vow with a ferocity that shocked the world. He slaughtered hundreds and thousands of *kshatriyas*, filling ten great lakes with their blood. He became known as the scourge of the warrior caste.

After the twenty first carnage, Parashurama became a teacher: he instructed many *brahmanas* in the art of war to check the rising domination of the warrior community.

From Priest to Prince

"It is easy for an impoverished *brahmana* like Parashurama to contain his desire for power than it is for a rich *kshatriya*," said many a cynic.

To prove them wrong, the lord descended upon earth as a prince who was willing to sacrifice everything for the sake of *dharma*. Rama — noble warrior, just ruler, dutiful son, loving brother, faithful husband — was the personification of virtue and rectitude, *maryada purushottama*, the lord's most august incarnation.

Vishnu as Parashurama, the unforgiving priest; Stone carving

Parashurama annhilates the warrior clans; Guler style miniature

Birth of Raghava-Rama

Dashratha, king of Ayodhya, scion of the Raghava dynasty, had three wives but no children. When he propitiated the gods, they gave him a sacred potion containing the essence of Vishnu.

After consuming this divine drink, the queens gave birth to four sons. Rama was the eldest, born to the noble Kaushalya. Next came Bharata, the son of the beautiful Kaikeyi. The youngest queen Sumitra gave birth to twins, Lakshmana and Shatrughna.

Rama's Virtue

Rama radiated a divine aura from an early age. His noble bearing and caring nature earned him the respect of young and old alike. Sages and scholars who visited the court of Dashratha were touched by his humility, dignity and grace. They spoke highly of this gentle prince of Ayodhya, of his respect for the laws of the land and his sense of duty.

Rama was but a boy when he learnt that the sage Vishvamitra was being tormented by the demons of the forest. He rushed to the *rishi*'s defence. With his arrows he kept the trouble-makers at bay while the sage performed his *yagna*.

Rama: Vishnu as the noble prince; Modern calendar print

41

Lakshmana and Sita following Rama into the forest; North Indian Miniature painting

When Rama heard how Ahalya had been turned to stone for being unfaithful to her husband, he was moved by compassion to redeem the hapless woman from her miserable fate. Such was the purity of his being that the touch of his foot washed away Ahalya's sin and liberated her to rejoin her husband.

Sita, the Earth-goddess

Rama broke a mighty bow that could not even be lifted by the gods and won the hand of Janaka's daughter, Sita, in marriage.

Sita was no ordinary girl. She was Bhoodevi incarnate. She had emerged from the earth when Janaka, king of Mithila, was tilling the sacred fields of the earth-goddess with his golden plough.

When Rama married Sita, Vishnu was reunited with his divine consort Lakshmi on earth.

The Exile

After Rama's marriage, Dashratha was so happy that he decided to pass on his crown to his eldest son and retire into the forest.

But he was stopped by Kaikeyi, his second queen, who said, "You once promised me two boons when I saved your life in a battle. I want them now: I want my son Bharata to be made your successor and I want Rama to live like a hermit in the forest for fourteen years."

Rama, Sita and Lakshmana on the banks of the river Godavari; North Indian Miniature

Rama, on learning this, discarded his royal robes and left Ayodhya dressed in clothes of bark, without regret or resentment.

"Let it not be said that a Raghava king does not keep his word or that a Raghava prince does not obey his father," he told his people who wept as he departed for the forest.

Bharata Rejects the Crown

Bharata, the son of Kaikeyi, refused to rule a kingdom procured through deception.

"I shall rule this land as my brother's regent until his return," he said placing Rama's sandals on the throne of Ayodhya.

Bharata, who also contained the spirit of Vishnu, lived like a hermit, outside the city, refusing to partake of the luxuries denied to Rama.

While these two brothers selflessly renounced their claims to the throne of Ayodhya, far away in the south, a battle raged between two brothers for the throne of Lanka: Ravana, ten-headed lord of the *rakshasa*s, finally drove his brother Kubera, lord of the *yaksha*s, out of Lanka and usurped his kingdom and his crown.

Then, mounting Kubera's flying chariot, the Pushpaka-*vimana*, Ravana rode across the cosmos indulging in an orgy of rape and plunder.

Rama comforts Sita during the forest exile; Pahari miniature painting

A Life of Misery

Rama meanwhile wandered deep into the forest, far from Ayodhya, followed by Sita, his dutiful wife. Lakshmana, his brother, joined them, serving Rama as Ananta-Sesha served Vishnu in Vaikuntha.

The forest was no sylvan retreat. Rama, Lakshmana and Sita had to continuously battle the elements, contending with wild beasts and hostile tribes.

Lakshmana cutting off Surpanakha's nose; Pahari miniature painting

Surpanakha Solicits Rama

In the final year of their exile, while they camped on the banks of the river Godavari, Ravana's sister Surpanakha cast her lustful eyes on Rama.

Rama turned her away. "I have a wife already," he said.

"This is the jungle, you take what you want." So saying Surpanakha attacked Sita intending to kill her and take her place.

"This is the jungle, you defend what is yours." So saying Lakshmana raised his sword and cut off Surpanakha's nose and ears.

Sita's Abduction

To avenge Surpanakha's mutilation, Ravana decided to abduct Sita. "With Sita gone, Rama will forget all about marital fidelity and take you as his wife," he assured his sister.

While Rama and Lakshmana were away on a hunt, Ravana approached Sita in the guise of a *rishi* with a request for alms.

Sita, too innocent to suspect a sage, welcomed him in keeping with the sacred laws of hospitality only to be dragged away to the island-kingdom of Lanka.

Ravana abducting Sita; Modern calendar art

Rama's Fidelity

Separation from Sita broke Rama's heart.

As he wept, Nature mourned with him: trees shed leaves, flowers lost their fragrance. The woods, once enlivened by the presence of Rama and Sita, became a gloomy place.

"Take comfort in our company," said the birds and beasts of the forests.

"I cannot. None can replace Sita," said Rama.

Realising he had hurt these innocent creatures by rejecting their affection, the lord said, "I will descend upon earth as Krishna who will be playfulness personified, *leela purushottama*. Then all of you can be my companions and dance and sing with me in the meadows of Madhubana."

Rama's Great Army

The birds and beasts of the forest promised to help Rama find Sita. Vultures flew high in the sky and monkeys scoured the earth until they found Rama's beloved on the island of Lanka locked in Ravana's pleasure-gardens.

The monkeys and bears of the forest led by the mighty Hanuman and the wise Jambuvan hurled sticks and stones into the sea to build a bridge to the island of *rakshasa*s. These were kept afloat by fishes, serpents, seals and other sea-creatures.

Thus did Vishnu rouse the forces of Nature to rescue his consort.

Ravana is Defeated

Rama strode across the sea on the bridge and launched an attack on Lanka with his monkey army.

They stormed the high walls, brought down the towers and set ablaze the palaces within. The *rakshasa*s

Rama, Lakshmana and Hanuman; Mysore painting

Rama killing Ravana; Palm leaf painting

with all their diabolical powers were no match for Rama's army of monkeys who had righteousness on their side.

Ravana watched in dismay the defection of his brother Vibhishana, the defeat of his mighty armies, the death of his brother Kumbhakarna and his son Meghanath at the hands of Rama and Lakshmana. But he was too proud to release Sita and make peace.

Finally, when all his resources had been exhausted, he rode into the battlefield himself and confronted Rama.

After a fierce battle, Rama, seated on Hanuman's shoulder, shot an arrow right through Ravana's heart. As the *rakshasa*-king fell, the monkeys and bears who had fought alongside Rama, yelled out in triumph.

Bhoodevi smiled. Her lord had saved her once again.

Sita is Rejected

Rama did not rejoice. He knew that the world had lost its innocence. Faith had been replaced by doubt.

When Sita was liberated from the pleasure-gardens of Lanka, Rama asked her to prove her fidelity. "Show the world that in body, mind and soul, you have been my faithful wife," he said.

Sita, surprised by Rama's order, walked through fire. The flames did not touch her. Agni, the fire-god, said, "I can burn only impure things. Sita is the earth, Bhoodevi herself, eternally pure. Nothing can pollute her."

But even Agni's words could not quell the vulgar suspicions in the hearts of men.

Faithful Husband

When Rama was crowned king of Ayodhya, his subjects refused to accept Sita as their queen. "How can she, who has lived under another man's roof, sit beside our king?" they asked.

Sita's trial by fire to prove her chastity; Mughal miniature painting

45

Rama, the dutiful king, in keeping with the wishes of his subjects, abandoned Sita in the forest. But when they asked him to remarry, he refused, "I exiled the woman you did not want as a queen. But she still remains my wife. I will remain eternally faithful to her," he said.

The gods praised Rama. "He is *ekam-patni-vrata*, true-to-one-wife," they said.

In the forest, away from the complications of worldly life, surrounded by gentle birds and beasts in the hermitage of sage Valmiki, Sita gave birth to Rama's sons: the twins Luva and Kusha.

Rama, meanwhile, performed his duties as a king with a golden image of Sita by his side. Though he had sacrificed personal joy, he made sure there was peace and prosperity in the lives of all his subjects.

Rama's Royal Horse

Years after his coronation, Rama's royal horse was let loose into the forest as part of the *ashwamedha yagna*. All the lands it traversed unchallenged came under Rama's suzreignity.

46 Rama, the noblest man to walk the earth; Tanjore painting

Vishnu and Lakshmi on
Ananta-Sesha; North Indian
miniature painting

47

When Rama's horse reached Sita's abode, it was captured by her twin sons. Luva and Kusha said "We will not accept the rule of a king who abandons his wife."

A great battle followed. The armies of Ayodhya tried their best to recover their royal horse but failed. They were no match for Sita's sons. Even Rama had to accept defeat.

"The power of *dharma* has enabled the sons of Sita to defeat the armies of Ayodhya," said the gods who advised the citizens of Ayodhya to accept Sita as their queen.

They agreed on one condition, "She must prove her purity once again."

Rama Returns to Vaikuntha

Tired of having her virtue questioned time and again, Sita said, "If I am pure let me return whence I came." Instantly the earth opened up and Sita descended into its depths.

The citizens of Ayodhya got their proof. But Rama lost his wife and with her went his will to stay on earth.

Sita with Luva and Kusha, sons of Rama who captured the royal horse of Ayodhya; Modern calendar art

Rama realised it was time to abandon Ayodhya and return to Vaikuntha. After appointing his sons as his successors, he bid farewell to the world of man, walking into the river Sarayu to free himself from his mortal body.

Mankind mourned Rama's departure for he was the embodiment of the ideal man; his reign, the Rama-*rajya*, was the most perfect ever.

Coronation of Rama; North Indian miniature painting

Vishnu Manifests as Krishna

Chapter VII

Bhoodevi's Complaint

In the Dvapara-*yuga*, the third-quarter of the world-cycle, the ambitions of kings burdened the earth. Bhoodevi stood before Vishnu in the form of a cow and cried: "Save me before the greed of man breaks my back."

Plucking two of his hairs, one white and one black, the lord said, "I will place these in the womb of Devaki, the Yadava princess, and she will give birth to your guardians, Baladeva and Vasudeva, who will rid the world of unrighteous men and reestablish *dharma*."

White-complexioned Baladeva and dark-hued Vasudeva, guardians of the earth; Orissan *patta* painting

Birth of Baladeva

Kamsa, lord of the Yadavas, had usurped the throne of Mathura by imprisoning his own father.

When oracles revealed that his sister, Devaki, would bear his killer, he had her thrown into the dungeons along with her husband Sura-Vasudeva. Every time she bore a son, Kamsa strode into the dungeon and brutally smashed the newborn's skull against the stony floor.

The gods came to the rescue of Devaki's seventh child. They drew him out of Devaki and placed him in the womb of Sura-Vasudeva's other wife Rohini who lived far away in Gokula in the house of Nanda, chief of cowherds.

Friend of Farmers

The child, conceived in Devaki and delivered by Rohini, was called **Baladeva**, the mighty one.

Always dressed in blue robes, this light-skinned incarnation of Vishnu, bearer of the pestle and the plough, was a friend of farmers. He taught them the art of tilling soil, dehusking grain and building canals. He was revered as **Sankarshana**, the cultivator.

Balarama, as he was sometimes called, loved taking care of fields and orchards or drinking wine and playing dice with friends; he despised the complicated politics of cities.

His ways were simple and straightforward, unlike those of his alter-ego, Vishnu's most perfect incarnation: Krishna.

Balarama: Vishnu as the lord of farmers bearing a plough; Mysore painting

49

Birth of Vasudeva-Krishna

Born of Vishnu's black hair, on a dark night, in the dark half of the lunar cycle when rainclouds rumbled across the sky and rains lashed the land of Vraja, Devaki's eighth child was a dark-hued boy, **Krishna**.

As soon as he was born, the gods cast the spell of sleep across Mathura so that unnoticed, Sura-Vasudeva could slip out of the city with his son in his arms.

Krishna being taken by Sura-Vasudeva across Yamuna to Gokula, the village of cowherds; Modern calendar art

Escape to Vrindavana

Vasuki, king of serpents, raised his mighty hood to shield father and son from the unrelenting rain. The river Yamuna parted its waters helping them reach Gokula safely. There, Sura-Vasudeva left Krishna in the care of the cowherd Nanda and his wife Yashoda.

When Kamsa learnt of the escape, he sent Pootana to kill every newborn in Gokula with the poison in her breasts. Krishna stopped this diabolical wet-nurse by suckling her to death.

Soon after, Nanda took Krishna to Vrindavana, a distant pastureland on the slopes of Mount Govardhana, far from Kamsa's murderous hands.

Yashoda's Adorable Child

In Vrindavana, adored by his foster-mother Yashoda, in the company of Rohini and Balarama, the lord delighted everyone with mischief and charm.

Only once did Krishna let Yashoda have a glimpse of his divinity. She saw him eating dirt but found in his mouth, not mud or dung, but the entire cosmos — the sun, the moon, the earth, the planets and the stars.

Stealing Butter

Krishna grew up with a fondness for butter and no attempt to keep it out of his reach was ever successful.

He would raid every kitchen and dairy in the village, helped by his brother and his friends, and then, with a smile, distribute his 'loot' amongst children and monkeys to the extreme annoyance of the milkmaids.

When caught, the bewildered expression on his butter-smeared face and his childlike protestations of innocence produced an upsurge of maternal affection in the *gopi*s that took them closer to the divine. In love, the women learnt to tolerate, even enjoy, the theft of butter.

Makhan-chor: Krishna, the adorable butter-thief; Mysore painting

Rasa-leela, the mystic dance of love and liberation in the meadows of Madhuban; North Indian miniature painting

Dance of Love

With his flute, Krishna captured the rhythm of the cosmos and infused idyllic surroundings — the river banks, pastures and fields — with romance and beauty.

Every night, charmed by his enchanting melodies and his winsome smile, the men and women of the village would abandon everything — ambition, jealousy, anger, lust, pride — and make their way to the flowery meadows of Madhubana to sport and play with the lord.

Krishna was the peacock, they were the peahens. As he played his flute, they danced to his tune, swaying gently around him until they all became one.

This was *rasa-leela*, the mystical dance of freedom and ecstasy.

Radha

Once, while the *gopi*s were bathing in the Yamuna, Krishna stole their clothes. Sitting on the highest branch of a tree, the lord smiled and said, "Let go of your inhibitions and stand before me without a facade."

Only Radha was willing to abandon everything — even honour, shame and pride — for the sake of Krishna. She asked for nothing in return.

The lord saw in this simple milkmaid the embodiment of perfect love. She became his dearest companion, the inspiration for his music. With Radha in his arms, Krishna danced in joyous abandon.

Krishna and his beloved Radha; Modern calendar art

51

Natawara: Krishna dancing on the hood of Kaliya, the serpent; South Indian bronze idol

Guardian of the Village

The peace of Vrindavana was often disturbed by Kamsa's minions: Agha, the python; Arista, the bull; Baga, the stork; Keshi, the horse; Vatsa, the heifer; Vyoma, the goat. Krishna and Balarama destroyed them all.

When a forest fire threatened Vrindavana, Krishna opened his mouth and consumed the flames.

He wrestled and subdued the deadly five-headed serpent Kaliya who had poisoned the waters of the village lake. To mark his triumph he danced on the serpent's hood and delighted the cosmos with his performance.

His footprint is still seen on the hood of cobras.

Divine Cowherd

Like all *gopa*s, Krishna looked after the cows of Vrindavan, leading them to their pastures at dawn and returning with them at dusk. Enchanted by the lord's music, the cows followed him readily and joyfully offered more milk.

During the festival of the rain-god Indra, Kamsa wished to sacrifice cows. Krishna protested against this practice.

"Killing cows to please Indra cannot benefit cowherds," said Krishna. "Let us instead worship a deity who looks after our welfare, like Mount Govardhana: it blocks rain-bearing clouds for our fields and provides grazing grounds for our cattle."

When the *gopa*s and *gopi*s accepted the lord's suggestion, Indra was so angry that he sent down torrential rains to drown the residents of Vrindavana.

Krishna killing the bull-demon (left) and the serpent-demon (right); Miniature paintings

52

To save his village and humble the rain-god's pride, Krishna raised Mount Govardhana with his little finger and turned it into a giant parasol under which cows, cowherds and milkmaids took shelter till the rains abated.

Govinda: Krishna holding up Mount Govardhana as a parasol to save the residents of Vrindavana from torrential rains; Rajasthani miniature painting

Invitation to Mathura

Krishna's many triumphs in Vrindavana made him famous across the three worlds.

Recognising him as his long-lost nephew, Kamsa sent the royal chariot to Vrindavana inviting Krishna and his brother Balarama to participate in the royal wrestling festival.

As Krishna mounted the chariot, the *gopa*s and *gopi*s wept in fear. "Kamsa's wrestlers will kill you. We may never see you again," they cried.

"It is I who shall kill Kamsa," said the lord, smiling reassuringly. "I will return and together we shall dance in triumph."

53

Krishna killing Kamsa;
North Indian miniature painting

Death of Kamsa

In the arena at Mathura, the brothers who had subdued many a wild bull on the streets of Vrindavana defeated the royal wrestlers effortlessly.

They won the admiration of the Yadavas for their strength and skill and were cheered as champions.

Kamsa, angered by their victory and popularity, lunged at Krishna. The lord grabbed him by the hair and dragged him across the ring until he was dead.

The Yadavas roared their approval.

Uddhava's Mission

After the death of Kamsa, the true identity of Krishna and Balarama as the sons of Devaki and Sura-Vasudeva became known to all. The citizens of Mathura readily welcomed the brothers into the royal fold.

Krishna sent the Yadava Uddhava to Vrindavana to inform his friends that he would not be returning to his village. "Tell them," said the lord, "It is time for Krishna to give up his pleasure-gardens — *vilasa-bhoomi* — and shoulder his responsibilities in his *karma-bhoomi*, the land of his destiny."

Uddhava carried with him Krishna's flute. Never again would the world hear Krishna make music, for his days as the carefree beloved of Radha had come to an end.

Sandipani's Son

Krishna and Balarama were sent to *rishi* Sandipani's ashram where they were taught every skill and scripture in just sixty-four days.

In gratitude, Krishna rescued his *guru*'s son from the clutches of the demon Panchaja who lived in a conch-shell in the bottom of the sea. After killing the demon, Krishna claimed the conch-shell as his trumpet, calling it Panchajanya.

The music of the conch-shell was a warning: the lord was now ready to kill the tormentors of the earth-goddess.

Mathura to Dwaraka

To avenge the death of his son-in-law Kamsa, Jarasandha, emperor of Magadha, sent his army to destroy Mathura. Krishna used his divine powers to transport the Yadavas, along with their families and wealth, to the city of Dwaraka that stood on an island in the western sea.

Krishna and his chief consort,
Rukmini; Contemporary painting

By withdrawing his kinsmen from Mathura, the lord prudently avoided bloodshed. In gratitude, Krishna was given the epithet **Ranchor-rai**, he-who-avoided-war.

Dwaraka became Vishnu's Vaikuntha on earth — the centre of *dharma*.

Krishna married eight noble women, chief of whom was Rukmini. Like the eight manifestations of Lakshmi, Krishna's queens were rulers of the eight quarters of his city.

Draupadi, a manifestation of the earth-goddess Bhoodevi, with her five husbands, the Pandavas, who embodied the five qualities of the perfect king; Pahari Miniature

Pandavas and Draupadi

Pleased to see Vishnu on earth in the form of Krishna, the earth-goddess Bhoodevi emerged from a fire-pit as Draupadi.

She wanted to marry an ideal king, but found none on the face of the earth. So she married the five Pandava princes of Hastinapur, Krishna's paternal cousins. Between them, the Pandava brothers had the five qualities of an ideal king: Yudhishtira possessed nobility, Bhima strength, Arjuna skill, Nakula charm, Sahadeva wisdom.

On Krishna's advice, the Pandavas, orphaned in childhood, asked their paternal cousins, the Kauravas, to give them their half of the ancestral kingdom.

They were given the undeveloped half — the wastelands of Khandavprastha — on which they built, with the help of Krishna, a rich and prosperous city called Indraprastha.

The Kauravas envied the Pandava fortune.

Sishupala Envies Krishna

The kings of the earth attended the coronation of Yudhishtira. During the ceremony, the Pandavas honoured Krishna. "You are to the Pandavas on earth what Vishnu is to Indra in heaven," they said.

Sishupala, king of Chedi, jealous of Krishna's rising reputation, stood up and shouted, "How dare the Pandavas treat a common cowherd as a royal guest?" He began abusing Krishna, calling him names.

A thousand times did Sishupala insult Krishna. A thousand times Krishna forgave him.

Then when he insulted Krishna one more time, Krishna said, "When you were born, I promised your mother to forgive you one thousand times. I have kept my promise. Now that you have crossed the limit, I shall punish you."

Having explained his intention, the lord hurled his discus, the Sudarshan-*chakra* and slit Sishupala's throat.

Krishna preventing the disrobing of Draupadi; Modern calendar art

The Game of Dice

Like Indra in the heavens, Yudhishtira became complacent surrounded by pomp and prosperity. Without consulting his benefactor Krishna, he accepted an invitation to a game of dice.

In the gambling hall he rolled the die and lost all he possessed: his kingdom, his brothers, even his own self.

His cousins, the Kauravas, the winners of the game, then asked him to wager Draupadi. Yudhishtira lost her too.

Draupadi was dragged by the hair into the gambling hall where the Kauravas decided to disrobe her in public.

Krishna Protects Draupadi

The kings of the world, witnesses of this tragedy, were too busy discussing the intricacies of the law and the rules of the game to come to Draupadi's aid.

Realising no man, neither husband nor king, would come to her rescue, Draupadi, with tears in her eyes, raised her arms towards the heavens and cried out, "Help me, Krishna."

Instantly the lord came to her rescue. For each robe that the Kauravas removed, there was another covering Draupadi.

No matter how hard they tried they could not strip the earth-goddess bare. When they gave up, Draupadi swore, "I will not tie my hair until I have washed it with the blood of the Kauravas."

Krishna promised to avenge her humiliation.

Justice and Peace

The Pandavas and their common wife, defeated in a game of dice, were driven out of Indraprastha. "You can claim your kingdom only after you live in the forests, without home or identity, for thirteen years," said the Kauravas, shutting the doors of civilisation on their face.

At first the Pandavas wished to attack and reclaim their lands immediately. "No, that will be against *dharma*. You lost the wager and so must suffer the exile," advised Krishna.

Thirteen years later, after much hardship, when the Pandavas returned from exile and asked for their kingdom, the Kauravas refused to part with it.

"This is against *dharma*," said Krishna. "The Pandavas kept their word. You must too."

"No," said the Kauravas.

"Give them at least five villages for the sake of peace," pleaded Krishna, willing to compromise to avoid bloodshed.

"No," said Duryodhana, the eldest Kaurava.

"Then you will get what you deserve — a war," declared Krishna, "And none will prevent the slaughter of the unrighteous Kauravas."

There is nothing in the three worlds that I need,
Nothing I do not own,
Nothing which I must get —
Yet, I labour forever

— Bhagavad Gita

Arjuna's Charioteer

As the Pandavas and Kauravas prepared for war, Balarama said, "Spilling blood for land or law makes no sense." He refused to fight for either side.

"If this war does not take place, *adharma* will reign supreme, and *pralaya* will destroy the world before its time is up," argued Krishna.

Krishna took up the reins of Arjuna's chariot. "Come Arjuna, help me establish *dharma* on earth."

Bhagavad Gita

Before the battle began, Arjuna lost his will to fight. He put down his weapons and cried, "How can I kill my own cousins for a piece of land?"

Parthasarathi: Krishna as Arjuna's charioteer, guiding him to face life's challenges instead of fearing them, a discourse which became renowned as *Bhagavad Gita* — song of the lord

Krishna showing his cosmic form to Arjuna; Modern calendar art

"This battle," said Krishna, "is not for your land or your crown; it is for *dharma*. You shall kill the unrighteous, not out of anger and vengeance, but because it is your duty. You are only an instrument of the divine being who rotates the cycle of life."

"Who is this divine being?" asked Arjuna.

"It is Vishnu," said Krishna, revealing his true self, his *vishvarupa*. "Behold, all that exists, exists within me; all that happens is because of me. Do not delude yourself into believing that it is you who create or kill. I am the cause of all events — the creator and the destroyer. Abandon yourself into my care, detach yourself from the result, and do as I say — I caused the war, I will decide its fate."

The words of Krishna became the song of the divine, the *Bhagavad Gita*, that made Arjuna see his actions in clear light.

Doubts cleared, intention clarified, decision taken, Arjuna picked up his bow and mounted the chariot. Krishna blew his conch and led Arjuna towards the enemy.

The Great War

The battle on the plains of Kurukshetra was no ordinary war; it was a battle to relieve the earth-goddess Bhoodevi of the burden of *adharma*.

Using every strategy of war, including guile, Krishna orchestrated the defeat of the unrighteous Kauravas. One by one, their commanders fell to the ground, struck by the ruthless sword of justice.

Defeat of Kauravas

On the final day of the war, encouraged by Krishna, Bhima killed Duryodhana, the leader of the Kauravas, striking him beneath the navel with his mace. This outraged the kings of earth who condemned Krishna for breaking the sacred rules of war.

"Where was this indignation when a helpless Draupadi was being abused by the Kauravas? Where was this sense of fair play when the earth-goddess Bhoodevi, burdened by your wickedness, begged for mercy? What use are your rules and laws when they do not uphold truth and justice?" asked the lord as he led the Pandavas to victory.

Deliverer

He who had brought love and laughter to the meadows of Vrindavana had filled the fields of Kurukshetra with the blood of unrighteousness kings and warriors.

Krishna blowing the conch Panchajanya and directing Arjuna to kill the unrighteous kings of earth

Draupadi, Bhoodevi incarnate, washed her hair with the blood of the Kauravas and tied her hair. "Nothing burdens the earth anymore, there is *dharma* everywhere," said the earth-goddess thanking Vishnu, her divine protector.

The fallen kings reviled Krishna.

The triumphant Pandavas cheered Krishna.

Krishna accepted it all, unfluttered by the rage, unflattered by the praise. Under his guidance, the Pandavas reestablished righteousness on earth.

Death of Krishna

But there was anger and sorrow in the heart of Gandhari, mother of the Kauravas. She cursed Krishna, "May you, like me, witness the degeneration and death of your kith and kin. And then, may you like an common beast die at the hands of a hunter."

Said Krishna, "Every action has a reaction. For the sake of *dharma* if I have to lose my family I am willing to pay the price."

Gandhari's curse was to come true years later.

The war had divided the Yadavas. Those who supported the Kauravas became sworn enemies of those who supported the Pandavas. Matters came to a head years later at Prabhasa where, after consuming too much liquor, there was an argument between the two groups. This led to a brawl. The brawl turned into a battle.

Krishna, like Gandhari, saw his sons, his grandsons, his great-grandsons, fight and kill each other in this civil war.

Krishna struck by a hunter's arrow as he rested under a banyan tree

Venugopala: Krishna, the divine cowherd, playing his flute and beckoning all creatures to join his cosmic dance; South Indian painting

Soon after, the sea rose and engulfed the city of Dwaraka.

In despair, Balarama renounced the world and let his life-breath slip out of his body in the form of a snake.

Having seen the Yadavas destroy themselves, Krishna sat under a banyan tree in contemplation. A hunter mistook his foot for the ear of a deer and shot a poisoned dart at him. As the poison took effect, the spirit of Vishnu left his earthly abode and returned to Vaikuntha.

Go-loka

The death of Krishna marked the dawn of Kali-*yuga*, the age of spiritual blindness.

"Have you abandoned us lord?" cried the *gopa*s and *gopi*s of Vrindavana.

Replied Vishnu, "How can I abandon those who love me? In Vaikuntha is *Go-loka*, the divine pleasure-garden. There, surrounded by celestial cows, under flowering trees, beside sparkling rivers, I play the flute and dance with Radha. Come, come and join me in my paradise, sing and dance around me for all eternity."

"How do we come there lord?"

"Work with wisdom and devotion, respect *dharma*, be compassionate, and you shall find the way to my garden of eternal delight."

Vishnu in *Go-loka*, the heaven where Krishna's beloved devotees can dance and sing with him for all eternity; North Indian embroidery

Vishnu Enlightens Mankind

Chapter VIII

Demons Corrupt *Vedas*

In Kali-*yuga*, the final quarter of the world-cycle, the *asuras* stole the *Vedas* and used their mystical secrets to become powerful beings. *Mantras* and *yagnas* were subverted for material gain, their spiritual aims disregarded.

The *sapta-rishis*, ancient keepers of wisdom, went to Vishnu and complained: "Nobody understands the *Vedas* anymore. Corrupted by the demons, they fail to direct man towards the divine. Save the texts before ignorance heralds the day of doom."

Mayamoha Deludes *Asuras*

Vishnu went to the kingdom of demons taking the form of a wily sage called **Mayamoha**, the deluder, with Garuda accompanying him as a monk.

Clean shaven, dressed in clothes of bark, with a begging bowl in hand, Mayamoha sat amongst the *asuras* denouncing the *Vedas*. "Don't waste your time with these high philosophies and complex rituals. They are nothing but superstitions. You don't need them to be powerful."

Vishnu as Mayamoha, the teacher who deluded demons into giving up the *Vedas*; Pahari painting

With clever arguments Mayamoha convinced the demons to abandon the Vedic way. They stopped chanting *mantras* and performing *yagnas*. They threw the holy texts out of their land and became heretics.

The *rishis* recovered the *Vedas* and began restoring them to their former glory.

The Divine Teacher

Meanwhile, on earth, the distortion of the *Vedas* by the demons had caused confusion: mankind had lost touch with the divine. Life lacked direction. There was suffering everywhere.

To fight this ignorance with knowledge, Vishnu descended upon earth as the enlightened teacher. Incarnating as Nara and Narayana, Kapila, Narada, Vyasa, Datta, Rishabha and Buddha, the lord taught man the true nature of the cosmos. He explained the mysteries of life and showed many ways to attain salvation.

Those who lived by his words found themselves in the paradise of Vaikuntha, attuned to the blissful rhythms of the cosmos. The rest, like demons, suffered the pangs of existence.

Tapas of Nara-Narayana

On the snowy peaks of the Himalayas, at Badrika, **Nara-Narayana**, two inseparable sages, performed terrible austerities, *tapas*. Nobody knew what they sought.

"Maybe they seek power," said the demon-king, Dambhodabhava. He sent hundreds of soldiers to attack them. The sages refused to fight. Instead, they hurled blades of grass which turned into fiery missiles killing everyone who dared disturb their serenity.

The god-king Indra sent hundreds of nymphs to seduce them. The sages remained unmoved. "We can create them ourselves." So saying Nara and Narayana rubbed their thighs and brought forth a voluptuous nymph called Urvashi, more alluring than all of Indra's *apsara*s put together.

"What do you want?" asked the gods and demons, unable to fathom the reason for their *tapas*.

"We seek the ultimate goal of existence — realisation and union with the divine spirit. Power and pleasure are merely temporal delights that will wither away someday," said Nara-Narayana.

Nara-Narayana, the twin incarnations of Vishnu; Temple carving

Kapila and *Jnana-yoga*

Kardama renounced worldly life soon after his son **Kapila** was born. A time came when Kapila decided to follow in his father's footsteps.

"Why did I lose my husband? Why am I losing my son?" wondered Devahuti, Kapila's mother, unable to come to terms with the separation.

Said Kapila, "Nothing is permanent in the material world. All that you see, smell, hear, touch or taste are material things, products of *prakriti*. They are transitory pleasures — here one moment, gone the next. If you want something permanent, you must look beyond the material reality and get in touch with the spiritual reality of the cosmos, the immutable *purusha*."

Kapila went on to explain the structure of the world. He enumerated the two principles which govern life: eternal soul and transitory substance.

This *Samkhya* philosophy became the corner-stone of mysticism and the foundation of intellectual introspection — *jnana-yoga*.

Kapila, the seer, who laid down the foundations of Indian mysticism; Pahari miniature painting

Narada and *Bhakti-yoga*

Even after performing a hundred thousand *yagnas*, King Prachinabarhis was not happy. "What have I done wrong? Why am I not content? Why do I experience no bliss?" he wondered.

The sage **Narada**, lute in hand, came forward to solve the king's problem. "With your rituals you are trying to control the world around you and make it work in your favour. But let me show you what you have really achieved."

Narada pointed to a vast field covered with the carcasses of cattle sacrificed in his many rituals.

"Your rites and rituals will never influence the workings of the world. But for killing these innocent beasts you will have to someday pay a terrible price."

Narada continued, "The desire to manipulate events in one's favour is unproductive because Vishnu, the supreme being, loves all creatures equally; he does not discriminate or favour anyone. Accept his divine intentions humbly and live life accordingly. Look at every event — good or bad — as the lord's gift, *prasada*, an opportunity to discover the divine. Only then will you realise his benign grace and live a life of joy."

Thus did Narada direct the king Prachinabarhis to the path of devotion called *bhakti-yoga* that leads straight to the heart of Vishnu.

Narada, the great devotee; South Indian bronze idol

63

Vyasa dictating the *Mahabharata* epic to Ganesha

Veda Vyasa and *Karma-yoga*

The sage Parashara fell in love with a fisherwoman called Satyavati as she ferried him across the river Ganga. She gave birth to his son **Krishna-Dwaipayana**, so called because of his dark complexion and because he was born on an island in the middle of the river.

Satyavati's son painstakingly compiled the *Veda*s, which had been lost to the world, with Ganesha, the lord of wisdom, serving as his scribe. His work made him famous in the three worlds as **Veda Vyasa** — compiler of the books of knowledge.

Krishna-Dwaipayana also wrote down the *Adi Purana* and the *Itihasa*, the book of myths and legends, through which he propogated the doctrine of duty, *karma-yoga*.

Said he, "Man must act according to *dharma* because *dharma* ensures harmony between the self and the world around. Actions motivated by desire unravel the cosmic fabric; they also generate emotions that trap

Dattatreya, the mendicant-teacher; Modern calendar art

one within the material world. *Nishkama karma*, selfless action focussed on duty not reward, enables one to attain salvation without having to renounce the world."

The followers of Vyasa became the first bards who revealed truth through tales of gods, king and sages.

Dattatreya, the Mystic

Anasuya, the wife of sage Atri, was renowned for her virtue. To test her, Vishnu arrived at her doorstep disguised as a sage and asked her to feed him unclothed. Anasuya, bound by the rules of hospitality, agreed to the strange request. But such was the power of her chastity that when she brought the food, Vishnu turned into an infant whom Anasuya fed as a mother, her virtue uncompromised. When Vishnu recovered his original form, he blessed Anasuya, "You will bear a son who will be the embodiment of Brahma, Vishnu and Shiva."

Thus was born Datta, the son of Anasuya. He was also known as **Dattatreya** after his father, the sage Atri.

Datta observed Nature carefully — the elements, the sun and the moon, birds and animals, men and women — and gained an insight into the nature of the world. Inspired, he went on to compose the *Avadhuta Gita* — the song of the recluse — that explains the doctrine of detachment, *vairagya*.

Through various occult sciences like *Tantra* and mystical disciplines like *Yoga*, Dattatreya taught mankind the means to yoke oneself to the way of the cosmos. His students called him the fountainhead of all knowledge, the supreme teacher, **Adinatha**.

He wandered around the world as a mendicant with his cow, Bhoodevi herself, and four dogs, embodiments of the *Veda*s. Said Dattatreya, "You can either remain ignorant and abuse Nature or you can learn from her and realise divinity."

Rishabha, the Ford-finder

Meru, wife of the noble king Nabhi of Ayodhya, dreamt of a mighty bull as she gave birth to her son. The prince was therefore named **Rishabha** — bull amongst men.

Rishabha ruled his kingdom wisely, teaching man seventy-two vocational skills and women sixty-four domestic arts.

He had many children. His daughter Brahmi invented the script called *Brahmi*. His son Bharata was a great king of India; after him the land continued to be known as *Bharata-varsha*, the kingdom of Bharata.

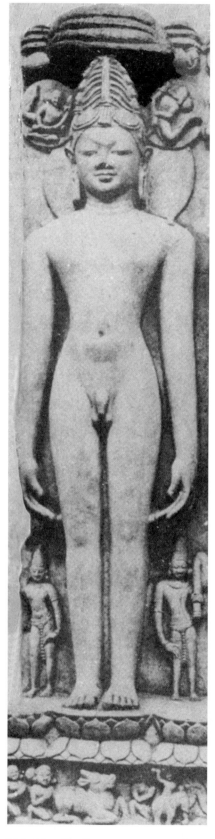

Rishabha, the *jina* or conqueror of bodily passions who built a bridge out of the wheel of existence, is described as an incarnation of Vishnu in some texts but this is not accepted by followers of the Jain faith; Stone idol on the walls of a Jain temple

65

When he had fulfilled his duties as a householder and king, Rishabha renounced worldly life. He crowned Bharata as his successor and went into the wilderness to live a life of austere contemplation.

Seated on Mount Kailasa, Rishabha reiterated the Jain philosophy, one of the oldest doctrines of liberation that enables man to break the fetters of *karma* and transcend *samsara*. Rishabha thus created a bridge out of the wheel of existence and became *tirthankara* — the ford-finder.

Buddha, the Enlightened One

Gautama, the Sakya prince of Kapilavastu, grew up surrounded by royal comforts adored by his loving mother. When he came of age, he married the beautiful princess Yashodhara. Within the walls of his palace there was nothing but joy.

But one day, as he rode through the city, he became aware of the suffering that plagues the life of every man — poverty, old age, disease and death.

He witnessed innocent animals and birds being mercilessly slaughtered by priests in elaborate ceremonies in the hope of relieving sorrow and ushering in joy.

In his compassion, Gautama decided to find the reason behind suffering. "Once I know what makes man unhappy, I will find a way to make him happy."

He renounced his wife and child, his wealth and crown and lived a life of a mendicant in the forest, fasting, meditating, talking to wise men, seeking a solution to the misery of man.

He sat under a pipal tree and refused to get up until he had found the answer. In time he did. He realised: desire was the root of all pain.

As **Buddha**, the enlightened one, Gautama concluded that to be free of desire one had to alter one's attitude towards the world and seek answers within oneself, through contemplation and restraint.

He propogated a disciplined way of life based on compassion known as Buddhism — the path of the enlightened.

Sakyamuni Gautama Buddha who found the answer to human suffering was considered to be an incarnation of Vishnu by some Vaishnavas though Buddhists refute this claim; Stone carving

Consort of Vishnu

Chapter IX

Vishnu's *Shakti*

On Vishnu's chest is a beautiful curl of golden hair called Shreevatsa. It is the symbol of Shree-Lakshmi, goddess of wealth and fortune, his consort.

When the goddess rose from the ocean of milk, she found only Vishnu — the detached guardian of the cosmos, the upright keeper of *dharma* — to be worthy of her affection. She became his *shakti*, source of his strength and splendour, invigorating him with her presence. Vishnu became **Shreenath**, her lord.

Vishnu is the soul of the universe; Lakshmi its substance. He is the protector; she the provider. They are the divine couple who nurture life.

Lakshmi Leaves Vaikuntha

Whenever Vishnu returned to Vaikuntha, tired after his battles with demons, Lakshmi would invigorate him with her affectionate touch.

Once, while Vishnu was resting, the sage Bhrigu entered Vaikuntha. Neither Vishnu nor Lakshmi saw him arrive. Insulted, Bhrigu kicked Vishnu on his chest shouting, "How can you sleep when someone is calling on you?"

Bhrigu's insolence horrified Lakshmi. To her surprise, the lord placed his hand on Bhrigu's foot and asked, "Did you hurt yourself by kicking me?"

The sage was touched by the lord's concern. Lakshmi was not. "Bhrigu kicked you on your chest, on Shreevatsa, and by doing so kicked me. Avenge this insult." She demanded angrily.

Lakshmi, goddess of wealth and fortune, who provides Vishnu with the wherewithal to preserve the world; Modern calendar art

Bhrigu kicking Vishnu on his chest; Comic book illustration

67

Vishnu and Lakshmi in loving embrace; Temple carving from Khajuraho, Madhya Pradesh

"I cannot harm one who is my guest," said the lord. Considering this an affront to her dignity, Lakshmi disappeared from Vaikuntha.

The Separation

Without Lakshmi beside him, Vishnu could not bear to live in Vaikuntha. He descended upon earth and waited for her under a banyan tree, refusing to move until she returned.

As time passed termites built a hill round him, covering his body completely.

Birds and beasts were stunned by the lord's plight. Cows rushed to the banyan tree and began shedding milk over the termite hill to nourish the lord. Touched by their devotion, Vishnu promised them eternal grace.

The Reunion

Bhrigu, the cause of Lakshmi's ire and Vishnu's anguish, was consumed by guilt. He took it upon himself to reunite the divine couple. He went near the termite hill and began kicking the cows.

The cows cried out and Vishnu rushed to their rescue, striking the offender with his mace.

"Ah, the lord has punished me for hurting Lakshmi whose spirit rests in every cow," shouted Bhrigu.

Hearing this, Lakshmi was pleased and she reappeared to join her husband in Vaikuntha.

Go-mata, the cow who nourishes the whole cosmos; Calendar print

Shreedevi finds the *parijata* tree in bloom while Vishnu is with Bhoodevi

Lakshmi's Promise

Lakshmi said to her lord, "Wherever you are in the three worlds, I shall always be by your side ."

"Should anyone try to take you away from me, I shall fight and win you back," said Vishnu.

When Vishnu descended upon earth, Lakshmi joined him as Rama's Sita and as Krishna's Radha and his Rukmini. And when the lord was **Yagna-purusha**, the god of sacrifice, she was Dakshina, goddess of charity.

Shreedevi and Bhoodevi

Vishnu's chief consort Shree-Lakshmi, goddess of power, fortune and splendour was fickle and demanding. In contrast, Vishnu's other consort, Bhoodevi, the earth-goddess, was faithful and submissive.

Both vied for Vishnu's attention.

When Indra gifted the *parijata* tree to Vishnu, both wanted it to be planted in their respective gardens, separated by a very high wall.

Bhoodevi, proud of her generative powers, argued that as she was the earth-goddess only she had the right to nurture the plant.

Vishnu gave her the celestial tree, but decreed that its flowers would always fall on the other side of the wall into Shreedevi's garden.

Shreedevi was delighted with her lord's decision. She taunted Bhoodevi, "The lord has given you the responsibility of the plant, while making sure it is I who derive real pleasure from it."

Vishnu, the benevolent lord, flanked by Shreedevi, goddess of heavenly fortune and Bhoodevi, goddess of earthly wealth; South Indian bronze idols

69

To humble Shreedevi, Vishnu said, "This plant will only bloom when I enter Bhoodevi's garden. Each time Shreedevi finds the *parijata* in bloom, she will have to endure the knowledge that her husband is with someone else."

Saraswati, Ganga and Yamuna

Saraswati, the goddess of knowledge, said, "Vishnu is **Vidyapati**, the patron of science, philosophy and the arts. Time and again he has rescued my children, the *Veda*s and the *Shastra*s, from demons. Surely he cares for me more than anyone else."

Ganga and Yamuna, the river-goddesses, disagreed. "Vishnu is **Jalashayin**, the keeper of the cosmic waters. He loves us most."

Lakshmi said, "The whole world knows Vishnu as **Madhava**, consort of Ma, that is me, the mother of the three worlds. He may be your guardian, but he loves none but me."

Vishnu with two consorts: Lakshmi and Saraswati, goddesses of wealth and wisdom; North Indian carving

The goddesses began arguing when the lord appeared before them and said, "Saraswati, the goddess of sound and speech, sits on the tip of my tongue. Ganga flows out of my right foot, Yamuna out of my left. Lakshmi resides in my heart."

Thus did Vishnu make peace with all the goddesses.

Abduction of Lakshmi

The demons once found Vishnu in deep meditation. "Let us carry Lakshmi away to *Patala*. With her by our side we will be rich and powerful," they said.

But when they brought Lakshmi to the nether-world, she began to weep and the *asura*s began experiencing great sorrow.

"So long as there are tears in the eyes of Lakshmi, there will be misery in *Patala*," revealed Shukra, preceptor of the demons.

"Why is she crying?" asked the *asura*s.

"You have wrenched her away from her lord. She can give you all the material comfort you want, but without Vishnu, she cannot give you any peace of mind."

Realising their foolishness, the demons let Lakshmi return to Vaikuntha. As she went away, they lost their wealth and power, but there was joy in their hearts.

Those who seek both spiritual bliss and material delight, worship both the lord and his consort, taking her name before his: 'Sita-Rama, Radhe-Shyam, Lakshmi-Narayana'.

70   Vishnu and Lakshmi in Vaikuntha; Rajasthani *haveli* painting

Son of Vishnu

Chapter X

Birth of Pleasure

Vishnu stands serenely detached from the material world, standing up for moral good and cosmic order. His consort, Lakshmi, on the other hand, provides the good things of the material life.

When they became one, they created Madana, the lord of pleasure, to show man and woman the wonders of life.

Madana's birth filled with world with joy. Nature came alive: flowers bloomed, birds sang.

His consorts, Priti and Rati, goddesses of love and longing, held aloft his banner and let the world see his insignia — the *makara* — symbol of growth and enrichment.

"I will make all creatures aware of *rasa*, the vitality of creation — its beauty, mystery and wisdom," said Madana.

Madana, lord of pleasure, shooting his love-darts while riding his parrot, a collage of damsels; Tanjore painting

Yearning for Life

Madana raised his sugarcane bow and shot flowery darts into the heart of every man and every woman, rousing their five senses, making them touch, taste, hear, smell and see the delights of the material world.

Suddenly *samsara* with its endless births and rebirths did not seem meaningless anymore; it was exciting, inspiring, intriguing. Man and woman learnt to enjoy life.

Intoxicated by Madana's arrows, the cosmos became a realm of pleasurable possibilities; in its vibrations, man and woman sensed the pulse of the divine.

Fear of Death

With the yearning for life, came the fear of death.

Tormented men and women asked Vishnu, "How do we live forever?"

The lord replied, "Nothing is eternal in this world. But all those who die will be reborn."

Vishnu revealed the procreative power of pleasure and became the guardian of embryos, to be invoked during the rites of conception, *garbhadhana-samskara*.

Madana, perched on a tree with his consort Rati, ready to shoot his love-dart; Pahari miniature painting

71

Auspicious *maithuna* images of man and woman on the walls of a temple

Divine Couple

Roused by Madana, man and woman experienced the fullness of life: its sublime and sensual nature.

Together they became *dampati*, keepers of homes. And every home, filled with their love, became a Vaikuntha, a safe haven where life is nurtured.

Maithuna images of man and woman in embrace, symbolising love, interdependence and completeness are therefore considered auspicious and placed on temple walls.

Andhaka's Lust

When the demon Andhaka cast his lecherous eyes upon the women of the world, the lord said, "Pleasure can delight the wise and lead him to divine ecstasy; it can also delude the fool and take him to his doom."

Taking the form of Mohini, the celestial enchantress, Vishnu multiplied himself a hundred thousand times until Andhaka could see ravishing nymphs wherever he looked.

Surrounded by so much temptation, Andhaka was driven to madness.

Virochana Cuts his Head

Virochana, king of the demons, considered himself to be the most powerful being in the three worlds.

On his way to conquer the heavens, he saw Mohini. Overwhelmed by desire, he abandoned his plan to fight the gods. Instead he began chasing the enchantress, begging her to be his wife.

"What will you give me if I agree?" she asked.

"Anything you want." promised Virochana.

"Give me your head," said Mohini. The demon immediately took his sword and beheaded himself.

Holding aloft the head of Virochana, Vishnu said, "Behold the fall of this mighty man — he sought to be master of the three worlds but failed to conquer his own desires."

Shiva Rejects the Material World

To transcend the wiles of *samsara*, Shiva, the celestial ascetic, shut his eyes, opening them only to destroy the world when it disturbed his meditation.

"Unless Shiva takes a wife, he will constantly be a threat to worldly existence," said Brahma.

Vishnu waited for a suitable opportunity to make Shiva participate in *samsara* without incurring his terrible wrath.

Mohini Saves Shiva

Shiva once unthinkingly gave the demon Vrika the power to burn anyone to death by the touch of his hand.

When the demon stretched out his hand to test his power on Shiva himself, Shiva realised his mistake and ran for his life. Vrika pursued him across the three worlds.

To rescue Shiva, Vishnu appeared as Mohini and distracted Vrika. Her inviting eyes made the demon forget all about the chase. "May I embrace you?" Vrika begged.

"You may, but only if you dance as I do," so saying Mohini began dancing. Vrika followed her every move, moving hand and limb as she did.

At one point, Mohini touched her head; Vrika, bewitched by the enchantress, did the same and burst into flames.

Shiva, the cosmic ascetic; Modern sculpture

Mohini: Vishnu as the celestial enchantress; Hoyasala stone carving from Karnataka

73

Hari-Hara-suta, the divine warlord, son of Shiva and Mohini; Modern calendar print

Mohini Charms Shiva

Shiva, the divine ascetic, became enchanted by Mohini's beauty. From their union came a *vira*, a brave knight, galloping on a white horse, waving a lance.

It was *Hari-Hara-suta*, the son of Shiva and Vishnu-Mohini. Known variously as Aiyanar, Velan, Ayyappa, Sastha, he helped gods fight demons and became guardian of human settlements.

Sati and Shiva

Drawn back into *samsara* by Vishnu, Shiva agreed to take a wife. He married Sati, daughter of Daksha, the great priest-king, and immersed himself so completely in conjugal life that he ignored the world around, even disregarding his father-in-law.

In retaliation, the proud Daksha organised a grand *yagna* inviting every creature in the cosmos except Shiva.

Enraged by her father's pettiness, Sati decided to disrupt the sacrifice. She rushed into Daksha's palace and leapt to her death in the sacred fire-altar so that the ritual, contaminated by her blood, ground to a halt.

Vishnu destroying Sati's corpse with his discus

Vishnu Destroys Sati's Corpse

Sati's death broke Shiva's heart. In fury, he raised his trident and beheaded Daksha. He then wandered across the galaxies carrying Sati's charred remains in his arms, unable to bear the agony of separation.

Watching Shiva weep, the denizens of the three worlds realised the terrible price of pleasure — pain. Shiva's sorrow disrupted the workings of the cosmos. To save the world, Vishnu let loose his Sudarshan-*chakra* and cut Sati's corpse into a thousand pieces.

"You have destroyed my Sati," cried Shiva.

"No," said Vishnu, "All I have destroyed is the body that had once ensheathed her soul. She will be reborn, for nothing in the material world is permanent, neither death nor sorrow."

Death of Madana

With Sati's corpse gone, Shiva became a hermit isolating himself in a dark cave. Sati, reborn as Parvati, princess of the mountains, tried in vain to draw him out. Finally, to rouse love in Shiva's heart she summoned Madana.

Madana's presence in Shiva's cave transformed the cold desolate abode of the hermit into a paradise for lovers, filled with the heady scent of spring flowers.

Madana shot a love-arrow at Shiva. But the ascetic was not amused. He opened his third eye and released flames of fury that reduced Madana to ashes.

A World Without Madana

Disturbed by the death of Madana, Vishnu said, "Behold the universe without the lord of pleasure: there is no *rasa*, no love, no joy, no beauty . . . *samsara* has become a wasteland."

"Madana deserved to die," argued Shiva. "He brought pleasure and pain to the world, binding all creatures to the flesh, distracting them from the divine."

"Madana simply revealed the possibilities of life — its beauty and bliss. Pain and disappointment stem not from his arrows but from the ego's refusal to accept the cosmic truth: all that comes must go."

Shiva killing Madana with the fire of his third eye; Kalighat painting

Madana Resurrected

Shiva saw the wisdom of Vishnu's words. Accepting the transitory nature of all things, he agreed to be part of worldly life.

Parvati, the princess of the mountains, was the chosen bride, Brahma the officiating priest. Vishnu, acting as the brother of the bride, gave her away.

Vishnu, considered in Tamil temple tradition to be Parvati's brother, giving her in marriage to Shiva; South Indian painting

75

The cosmos rejoiced.

On the icy peaks of Kailasa, as Shiva rediscovered love, Madana was reborn. The twang of his bow was heard across the cosmos once more.

Madana to Mohana

Though resurrected after his tryst with Shiva, Madana remained invisible. He existed in spirit as Ananga, the bodiless one.

Rati and Priti, the consorts of Madana, could not bear the thought of never gazing upon their lord's handsome face.

Moved by their lamentations, Vishnu said, "The world will rediscover the delight of Madana in its purest form in Krishna. *Go-loka* in Vaikuntha will be the new pleasure-garden where Krishna as the cosmic beloved, **Mohana**, will enchant all with the music of love. The fun, the frolic, the joy of rain-drenched days and moonlit nights will all be there. Only *rati-krida*, the dance of amorous embrace will be elevated to *rasa-leela*, the dance of divine union, while *bhukti*, the unrestrained pleasures of Madana will transcend into *bhakti*, the ecstatic devotion for Krishna."

Madana on his parrot; Temple carving

Krishna, the new love-god known as **Madanamohana**, he-who-can-charm-Cupid; Miniature painting

Companions of Vishnu

Chapter XI

Sesha and Garuda

Vishnu's paradise, Vaikuntha, is the pivot of the cosmos. It stands on the ocean of milk, radiant with golden spires, sparkling gems and bright banners. Here Vishnu, ruler of the universe, holds court with Lakshmi by his side, ensuring that *dharma* is respected by one and all.

When order prevails, Vishnu rests in peace on the coils of Ananta-Sesha, the divine serpent.

When *dharma* is threatened, Vishnu rides into battle on the celestial bird Garuda to set things right.

Kadru Enslaves Vinata

Sesha and Garuda were both sons of Kashyapa, the celestial sage, by his wives Kadru and Vinata.

Kadru, mother of serpents, once said that Ucchaishrava, the divine stallion, had a black tail.

Vinata, mother of birds, believed the celestial horse was spotlessly white. She was so confident that she chirped, "If you can prove that Ucchaishrava has even a single black hair on its tail, I will be your slave."

Kadru secretly summoned her children and hissed, "Go and cling to the tail of Ucchaishrava as it rides past the horizon at dawn tomorrow." The serpents obeyed so that the next day, from afar, the divine horse appeared to have a black tail.

By this deceit, Kadru won the wager and made Vinata her slave.

Sesha Becomes Vishnu's Throne

Sesha, eldest of the serpents, did not approve of his mother's trickery. He broke all ties with his siblings and his conniving mother.

Sesha's nobility so pleased Kashyapa that he said, "You will be the support of the cosmos. Your mighty hood will be the foundation of the universe. On your coils will rest the lord of the world, Vishnu himself."

Garuda Steals *Amrita*

Kadru meanwhile demanded the elixir *amrita* as the price of Vinata's freedom.

So the eagle Garuda, mightiest of Vinata's sons, swooped down upon Amravati, the city of the gods, in search of

Garuda, the solar bird with golden wings who rules the sky; Deccan stone carving

Ananta-Sesha, the serpent with many heads who supports the earth; Deccan stone carving

Ucchaishrava, the white horse of the gods, appeared to have a black tail because serpents, children of Kadru, clung to it

the celestial drink. He found it in a well of fire guarded by two huge dragons.

Garuda flapped his great wings to put out the fire, pecked the dragons to death and flew off with the pot of elixir. Indra tried to stop him with his dreaded thunderbolt, the *vajra*, but it barely managed to singe one of the mighty bird's feathers.

Garuda Tricks Kadru

Having secured the release of his mother with the stolen nectar, Garuda told Kadru and her sons, "You must not drink divine nectar with unwashed lips."

The serpents saw sense in Garuda's advice. They rushed to a nearby river to wash their mouths leaving the pot of nectar unguarded on the river bank.

While they were away, Garuda summoned Indra to reclaim the pot of *amrita* and take it back to the heavens.

Thus did Garuda manage to free his mother without letting the serpents take a sip of nectar.

Garuda Becomes Vishnu's Mount

"Why did you not sip the *amrita* yourself?" asked Vishnu.

Garuda replied, "I do not take what is not mine."

Pleased with this reply, Vishnu said, "Your nobility matches your brawn and brain. Would a worthy bird like you consider being my mount?"

"Only if you let serpents become my natural food," requested Garuda.

"So be it," said Vishnu.

Garuda became Vishnu's *vahana* and his insignia, appearing on the lord's banner.

Jaya and Vijaya

There are seven gates round Vaikuntha. Those who renounce lust, anger, greed, pride, attachment and envy can cross the first six. At the seventh stand the doorkeepers Jaya and Vijaya permitting entry to only those who have transcended the fear of death and the passion for life.

Sanaka, Sananda, Sanatana and Sanatkumar, renounced the world as soon as they were born and decided to go Vaikuntha. But they were stopped at the gates by Jaya and Vijaya who said, "How can we let you enter, you who have had no taste of life or death?"

Garuda, Vishnu's mount and the eternal enemy of serpents; stone carving from South-East Asia.

Sanata-*kumar*s, the four child sages saluting Vishnu; Modern calendar print

Three times did the children try to enter Vaikuntha; three times they were stopped by Jaya and Vijaya.

Piqued, the four *kumar*s cursed the divine doorkeepers, "You have, like demons, blocked our spiritual journey into the abode of the lord. May you therefore become *asura*s three times over."

Vishnu rushed to the gates of Vaikuntha to console Jaya and Vijaya who were only doing their duty. Said the lord, "Even as demons, you will be my gatekeepers, embodying the six emotions that shut the doors of Vaikuntha. I will fight you, destroy you and show man the road to my paradise."

Jaya and Vijaya were reborn as the lustful Hiranyaksha, the wrathful Hiranyakashipu, the greedy Kartaviryarjuna, the proud Ravana, the obsessive Kamsa and the jealous Sishupala who were killed by the lord in his incarnations as Varaha, Narasimha, Parashurama, Rama and Krishna.

Jaya and Vijaya, the door-keepers of Vaikuntha; Modern calendar print

Vishnu-*doota*s Rescue Ajamila

Ajamila lived a wanton life, drinking, gambling, disrespecting elders and neglecting his family. As he lay dying, he called out to his son: "Narayana, Narayana, please come here."

The boy paid no heed to his father's request.

He shouted again, "Narayana, Narayana, please come here." The boy still did not come. And so Ajamila breathed his last, mumbling "Narayana, Narayana."

Yama, the god of death, decided that Ajamila who had done not one good deed in his entire life should spend the rest of eternity suffering in hell.

As his dreaded Yama-*doota*s rushed towards Ajamila's corpse to collect his soul, they were stopped by Vishnu-*doota*s, the lord's angels who said, "By chanting the name of Narayana in his last moments, Ajamila has performed one pious act and must therefore be given a chance to redeem himself."

The two groups of divinities fought until the will of Vishnu prevailed. Ajamila was allowed to be reborn.

In gratitude, Ajamila spent his next life in piety, continence, charity and reverence making up for all that he had done in his previous existence. Ultimately he was given salvation, and allowed to reside in the blissful heart of Vishnu.

Lord Vishnu with his consort Lakshmi and two Vishnu-*doota*s; Pahari miniature painting

The Quarrel-monger

Lute in hand, chanting, "Narayana, Narayana," the divine sage Narada went across the three worlds spreading rumours, causing rifts.

In Vaikuntha, he would regale his lord Vishnu with his merry tales. "I described Ahalya's beauty to Indra until he began lusting for that married woman . . . Daksha hates Shiva after I reported how Shiva ridicules him . . . I spoke about Jamadagni's cow with so many superlatives that Kartaviryarjuna wants to steal it now . . . I made Shreedevi jealous of Bhoodevi . . . I put the fear of death in the heart of Kamsa . . . I praised the pompous Ravana into believing that he was greater than the gods . . ."

"Why do you do this, Narada?" asked Vishnu.

"Do what?"

"Cause so much trouble."

"I don't do anything. I merely test their faith in you. If they were truly your devotees, would any of them be lustful, wrathful, greedy, envious, frightened or proud?"

Vishnu burst out laughing and blessed his dearest devotee who kept chanting, "Narayana, Narayana".

Narada regaling Vishnu with his tales; Pahari miniature painting

80

Images from Puri, Orissa, of Vishnu
as Krishna-Jagannatha (middle) with
his elder brother Balabhadra (top)
and younger sister Subhadra
(bottom); *Patta* painting

81

Narada saluting Vishnu; Pahari
miniature painting

Narada Learns About *Maya*

"The world is my *maya*. He who accepts this, realises me," said Vishnu.

"What is *maya*?" asked Narada.

"Before I reply, will you fetch me some water?" requested the lord pointing to a river.

Narada did as he was told. But on his way back, he saw a beautiful woman. Smitten by her beauty, he begged the woman to marry him. She agreed.

Narada built a house for his wife on the banks of the river. She bore him many children. Loved by his wife, adored by his sons and daughters, Narada forgot all about his mission to fetch water for Vishnu.

In time, Narada's children had children of their own. Surrounded by his grandchildren, Narada felt happy and secure. Nothing could go wrong.

Suddenly, the sky was covered with dark clouds. There was thunder, lightning, rain. The river rose in flood, broke its banks and washed away Narada's house, drowning everyone he loved, everything he possessed. Narada himself was swept away by the river.

"Help, help. Somebody please help me," he cried. Vishnu immediately stretched out his hand and pulled Narada out of the river.

Back in Vaikuntha, Vishnu asked, "Where is my water?"

"How can you be so remorseless? How can you ask me for water when I have lost my entire family?"

Vishnu smiled. "Calm down, Narada. Tell me, where did your family come from? From me. Where has to gone? Into me. I am the only reality, the only entity in the cosmos that is eternal and unchanging. Everything else is an illusion — a mirage, constantly slipping out of one's grasp. You, my greatest devotee, knew that. Yet, enchanted by the pleasures of worldly life, you forgot all about me. You deluded yourself into believing that your world and your life was all that mattered, that nothing else was of any consequence. As far as you were concerned the material world was infallible, invulnerable, perfect. That is *maya*."

Mayin: Vishnu, the lord of all illusions; Modern calendar art

82

Devotees of Vishnu

Bhakti, loving devotion for the lord, defines the path to Vishnu's heart and is the key to Vaikuntha. Popular tales of *bhakti* speak of Vishnu's response to the cry of the true devotee — be it a distraught child or a helpless beast — and reaffirm that belief.

Parikshit Faces Death

King Parikshit, parched after a long day's hunt, entered a hermitage and asked for some water. When the hermit, who was lost in meditation, did not respond, Parikshit became so angry that he threw a dead snake round the hermit's neck.

For this misdeed, the hermit's disciple cursed Parikshit that he would die of a snake bite within seven days.

On learning of the curse, Parikshit rushed back to his city, hid in a tower and ordered his guards to kill every snake in his kingdom.

But nothing could take away his fear of death. Plagued by nightmares, Parikshit sought the advice of the gods.

"Listen to the tales of Vishnu and you will overcome your fears and learn to appreciate the few hours of life at hand," they said.

Parikshit invited his bards who recounted the wonderful tales of Vishnu and his many incarnations. As the hours rolled by, Parikshit realised the value of discipline, patience, righteousness and love. No more did he suffer the pangs of guilt, shame and regret. He came to terms with his life and his accomplishments.

When the seventh day dawned, Parikshit faced the serpent of death without fear.

Dhruva's Unshakable Devotion

Suruchi, favourite queen of King Uttanapada, on finding her five-year-old step-son Dhruva sitting on the lap of her husband, pulled him down shouting, "Only my son has that right, not you or anyone else."

Dhruva began to cry. His mother Suniti, long neglected by Uttanapada, tried to console him saying, "More valuable than your father's love is the eternal love of Vishnu, divine father of the whole universe."

Dhruva left his father's palace and went into the forest where he performed austerities to win the love of Vishnu.

Chapter XII

Parikshit listening to tales of Vishnu; Pahari miniature painting

Dhruva seated on Vishnu's lap

83

The intensity of his penance alarmed the gods. They tried to distract him from his goal but to no avail.

Moved by Dhruva's steadfast resolve, Vishnu placed the child lovingly on his lap and said, "No one will ever pull you down from here."

Dhruva, eternally seated on Vishnu's lap, became the pole star, the celestial body that can never be moved from its position.

Vishnu Saves Gajendra

While sporting with his herd in a lotus-lake, Gajendra, the king of elephants, disturbed a mighty crocodile who grabbed one of his legs and began pulling him under the water.

Trapped within the crocodile's strong jaws, Gajendra tried in vain to free himself. He struggled hard but the crocodile's hold remained as firm as ever.

Gajendra called out to his herd, but they were too frightened to come to his aid.

Vishnu liberating Gajendra, the elephant-king, from the jaws of the crocodile; Temple wall carving

As he was about to drown, the elephant-king picked up a lotus with his trunk. Lifting it towards the heavens, he cried, "I offer this to Vishnu, my lord, the refuge of the helpless."

Instantly, the lord descended from Vaikuntha on his mount Garuda, and liberated Gajendra by striking down the crocodile with his discus.

Heart of Hanuman

Hanuman, the monkey, was one of Rama's greatest devotees.

Once he was given a pearl necklace by Sita. With typical simian curiosity, he broke the necklace and began examining each pearl. "What are you doing?" asked the citizens of Ayodhya.

"I am looking for Rama in this pearl," he said.

The citizens of Ayodhya burst out laughing. "Foolish monkey, Rama is on his throne, not in that pearl," they said.

Hanuman said, "That is not true. Rama is Vishnu and is present everywhere — in the rocks, in the trees, in the sky, even in my heart."

"Really, then show us your heart. Let us see if Rama resides in you."

Hanuman tore his chest open with his bare hands. Inside, on his heart, the citizens of Ayodhya saw to their amazement the divine image of Rama.

Hanuman showing Rama's image on his heart; Modern calendar art

Krishna's Hunger

On a hot summer day, Krishna had strayed far away from his village. Tired and hungry, he came upon some sages performing a grand *yagna* on the banks of the river Yamuna. They were pouring pots of clarified butter and baskets of fruits into the sacred fire, chanting hymns in praise of the gods.

"Why don't you give me the food, instead of burning it in that fire? I am hungry," said Krishna.

"Go away, go away, you uncouth cowherd," cried the priests as they continued with the sacrifice.

Krishna went away. But as he was passing the houses of the priests, their wives saw him and said, "Dear child, you look hungry. Come in and eat."

The women fed Krishna with their own hands. The lord said, "You will attain salvation because there is more merit in your love and generosity than in rituals that lack compassion."

Krishna being fed by wives of priests; Pahari miniature painting

Bhairava drinking Vishnu's blood

Vishnu Offers his Blood

Infuriated by man's wickedness, Shiva became the fierce Bhairava on a rampage, killing, ripping out hearts and drinking blood, his menacing laughter thundering all around.

Vishnu went to Bhairava and pleaded on behalf of man.

Bhairava said, "I will go on killing until my bowl is filled with enough blood to quench my thirst." It was common knowledge that Bhairava's bowl could never be filled and that his thirst could never be quenched.

"Let me give you all the blood you need. You don't have to bleed mankind." So saying, Vishnu struck his forehead with his sword and let his blood spurt into Bhairava's bowl.

Aeons passed, Vishnu kept pouring his blood into the bowl. Bhairava kept drinking it.

Bhairava realised that Vishnu was sacrificing himself for the sake of the world. Moved by Vishnu's generosity, Bhairava declared, "So long as you preserve the world, I will not seek to quench my thirst. But when the world becomes so corrupt that even you cannot sustain it, I will raise my trident and squeeze every drop of blood from the heart of man."

86

Incarnations of Vishnu

It is said that when Vishnu revealed his entire self, his *vishvarupa*, such was his magnificence that a thousand suns paled before his splendour, the earth shook, oceans dried up, gods trembled in awe.

The presence of such an all-powerful all-encompassing divinity can overwhelm man. So the lord, in his benevolence, has chosen to present himself in forms that man can comprehend and identify with. These are his *avatars*.

Dasha-avatar

Vishnu is identified mainly through ten forms — the *dasha-avatar* — that he took to save the world. These incarnations are:

Matsya — the one-horned fish

Kurma — the mighty turtle

Varaha — the fierce boar

Narasimha — the man-lion

Vamana — the clever dwarf

Parashurama — the vengeful warrior-priest

Rama — the dutiful prince

Krishna — the righteous cowherd

Buddha — the compassionate reformer

Kalki — the messiah

Some exclude the Buddha, and **Balarama**, the elder brother of Krishna, is named instead.

Evolution of Ten Incarnations

The sequence of the *dasha-avatars* reflects the biological evolution of man from marine life (the fish Matsya) through amphibians (the turtle Kurma) and terrestrial beasts (the boar Varaha) to half-humans (the man-lion Narasimha), malformed humans (the dwarf Vamana) and finally perfect man.

Amongst the human *avatars* the sequence reflects changes in social attitudes from conformism through rebellion to reform and finally, rejection.

Parashurama is a *brahmana*, Rama a *kshatriya*, members of the higher castes fighting to uphold ancient moral and ethical values. Krishna, a common cowherd, challenges obsolete and ineffective laws. The Buddha rejects rituals that fail to satisfy the needs of man, while Kalki, the messiah, offers liberation from this imperfect world and salvation in the next.

Krishna, the most popular incarnation of Vishnu is considered to be the lord's supreme and complete manifestation

Number and Identity of *Avatars*

Though traditionally, Vishnu is associated with only ten incarnations, the number and identities of these *avatars* varies from text to text.

In *Bhagavata Purana*, there are twenty-four incarnations; in *Devi Bhagvatam* there are twenty-six.

In the Thai epic, *Narayana Sippang*, popular in South East Asia, there is no mention of Parashurama, Buddha or Kalki. The list of ten *avatars* has in their place three other incarnations: the buffalo who gored a buffalo-demon to death; the damsel, who tricked a demon into killing himself; and the false teacher, who fooled the demons of Tripura into abandoning the worship of their guardian deity.

Some incarnations, the *poorna-avatars*, like Rama and Krishna, are believed to possess the lord's divine personality in its entirety. The rest, the *amsa-avatars*, possess it either temporarily or partially.

Dasha-avatara, ten incarnations of Vishnu: 1. **Matsya** 2. **Kurma** 3. **Varaha** 4. **Narasimha** 5. **Vamana** 6. **Parshurama** 7. **Rama** 8. **Balarama** 9. **Krishna** 10. **Kalki** excludes Buddha but includes Balarama; Modern calendar print

1	2	3
4		5
7		8
6	9	10

Vishnu in *Go-loka* surrounded by his ten incarnations that includes Buddha but excludes Balarama:
1. **Matsya** 2. **Kurma** 3. **Varaha**
4. **Narasimha** 5. **Vamana**
6. **Parshurama** 7. **Rama** 8. **Krishna**
9. **Buddha** 10. **Kalki;**
North Indian wall painting

Vishnu beheading Pulomi, mother of sage Shukra

Vishnu Kills Pulomi

In the *Matsya Purana*, Vishnu is said to have three celestial incarnations — Narayana, Narsimha and Vamana — and seven human *avatar*s. According to this sacred text, the gods once attacked the demons, while their *guru* Shukra was away. The *asura*s, helpless without their preceptor, sought the aid of Pulomi, Shukra's mother. "I will cast a spell of sleep on the gods until my son returns," she said. Before she could utter the magic formula, Vishnu severed her neck with his dreaded discus, the Sudarshan-*chakra*. To atone for the crime of killing a woman, Vishnu had to take birth as a human being seven times over as Datta, Mandhata, Parashurama, Rama, Vyasa, Buddha and Kalki.

The Buddha mentioned here and in many other *Purana*s is not the fountainhead of the Buddhist religion. He is identified with Mayamoha, the wily teacher who tricked demons into giving up the *Veda*s.

Lesser Known Incarnations

Some of the lesser known *avatar*s are:
Yagna — the embodiment of sacrifice
Dhanvantari — the celestial physician
Dharma — the bull of righteousness
Mohini — the enchantress
Hamsa — the wise swan
Hayagriva — the horse-headed warrior
Sanat-*kumar*s — the four child-sages
Nara-Narayana — the twin practitioners of *tapas*
Dattatreya — the teacher of *Yoga* and *Tantra*
Narada — the champion of *bhakti*
Vyasa — the compiler of the *Veda*s
Kapila — the propounder of *Samkhya* philosophy
Rishabha — the *tirthankara*
Prithu — the domesticator of earth
Mandhata — the establisher of *varna-ashrama dharma*

Hayagriva, the horse-headed Vishnu is rarely mentioned in the list of *avatar*s; Mysore painting

Vishnu's innumerable incarnations protected mankind through incalculable crises, though his divine presence was not noticed or acknowledged every time.

Concept of *Vibhuti*s

Closely associated with the concept of *avatar*s is the concept of the *vibhuti*.

While every creature possesses a spark, *tejas*, of the divine, only those who fully express this divine potential come to be identified with the lord and become worthy of worship. These are Vishnu's *vibhuti*s.

They include: the most resonant vibration, 'Aum'; the most benevolent symbol, the *swastika*; the perfect hymn, Gayatri; the bravest god, Indra; the noblest demon, Prahlada; the wisest sage, Narada; the greatest patriarch, Daksha; the finest cow, Surabhi; the prime element, fire; the most luminous celestial body, the sun; the most venomous serpent, Vasuki-Sesha; the most beautiful season, spring; the highest mountain, Meru-Mandara; the strongest stone, *shalagrama*; the fastest horse, Ucchaishrava; the greatest bird, Garuda.

Vishnu thus resides in all that is perfect, wise, beautiful and good, eternally bringing hope, peace, stability and joy to the three worlds.

Aum, the sacred chant which contains the spark of Vishnu; Kangra miniature

Vishnu on Garuda; Wood idol from Bali

91

Attributes of Vishnu

Panchajanya Sankha
Conch-Shell

Nandaka
Sword

Kaumodki Gada
Mace

Sudarshan Chakra
Discus

Parashu
Axe

Saranga Dhanush
Bow

Kamala
Lotus

Mayurpankh
Peacock Feather

Bansuri
Flute

Yashudanda
Sugarcane

Go-mata
Cow

Go-pada
Cow's footprint

Mukuta
Crown

Makara-kundala
Fish-earrings

Kaustubha
Wish-fulfilling
gem

Tulsimala
Necklace of tulsi
leaves

Vaijayanti
Jewelled Garland

Vanamala
Garland of wild
flowers

Janayu
Sacred-Thread

Shrivatsa
Curl of hair on
chest

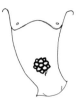
Padmanabha
Lotus on navel

Pitambara
Yellow Dhoti

Urdhva-Pundra
Sacred Mark

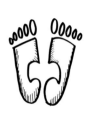
Vishnupada
Sacred footprint

Shuka
Parrot

Kurma
Turtle

Meena
Fish

Makara
Capricorn

Shalagrama
Stone

Vatapatra
Banyan Leaf

Ananta-Sesha
Serpent Couch

Garuda
Eagle-mount

Garuda-dhvaja
Flag

Yagna-kunda
Fire-altar

Tulsi
Sacred basil

Swastika
Auspicious Symbol

92

Attributes of Vishnu

Vishnu is associated with certain features that distinguish him from other gods. Focussing on his role as the preserver of life, these attributes are not be taken literally; their symbolic meanings grant devotees a profound insight into the sublime nature of the lord.

Physical traits

Vishnu's charm and beauty — his lotus shaped eyes, winsome smile, thick long hair, broad shoulders, lithe limbs and dark complexion — rouses love in devotees and passion in poets. They reflect *rasa* — life's mystery, beauty and awe.

Vishnu is blue as the sky, and like the sky always watches over the earth. He is dark as the rain-clouds whose presence brings joy after the hot dry days of summer. Like the colour black, Vishnu is omnipresent, seen even in the dark.

His four arms represent the four directions of the cosmos that he supports at all times.

On his chest is a characteristic tuft of hair called Shreevatsa — the symbol of Shree-Lakshmi, his consort, who is the goddess of life, protected and loved by him.

Brahma, the creator, sits on a lotus that springs from Vishnu's navel. This is the primal lotus that bloomed when life began.

Vishnu is known across the three worlds for his smile that is at once seductive and mysterious. The smile radiates happiness and celebrates the delights of worldly life. It also mocks man who, obsessed with his ego, has lost sight of the divine. And for all the troubled souls of the cosmos, the smile of the lord offers reassurance and love.

Garments and Jewellery

Vishnu adorns his dark body with bright yellow robes, the *pitambar*, as he plays the role of **Surya-Narayana**, the sun-god, who radiates warmth and light.

His earrings are shaped like a *makara*. *Makara*, or capricorn, is a fabulous sea-monster: part-fish, part-goat, part-elephant. Some describe it as a dolphin or a crocodile. It is the insignia of Vishnu's son, Madana, lord of desire, union and growth. When Madana's body was destroyed by Shiva's third eye, his spirit entered Vishnu who took over his functions, presiding over the life-giving rites of conception symbolised by these characteristic earrings.

Vishnu with the mark of Lakshmi — Shreevatsa — on his chest; South Indian idol

Vishnu and Lakshmi on Garuda; South Indian idol

Vishnu's conch (right), sacred mark (centre) and discus (left)

Vishnu wears a jewel called Kaustubha either round his neck or on his crown. This jewel, also called Chintamani or Parasmani, is a wish-fulfilling gem that rose from the ocean of milk and is said to symbolise the sun.

As Krishna, the celestial peacock who enchants his devotees with his divine dance, he wears a peacock feather on his crown.

Vishnu has two garlands round his neck: the jewelled Vaijayanti, that acknowledges his many triumphs over demons, and another, the Vanamala, made of wild flowers, that symbolises love which binds him to his devotees.

Weapons

Vishnu seated on the coils of the cosmic serpent Ananta-Sesha (left) when *dharma* is upheld; Vishnu riding on the wings of the celestial eagle Garuda (right), ready to do battle when *dharma* is threatened; Stone carvings

Vishnu is a warrior god, constantly fighting darkness, *tamas*, using light, *jyoti*. He battles the forces of *adharma*, that threaten the stability of the world, using many

94

weapons: Kaumodaki, the mace; Sudarshana, the discus; Nandaka, the sword; Sharanga, the bow; Parashu, the axe. Vishnu, bearer of these five weapons, is known **Panchayudha**.

A demon called Gada was renowned for his charitable nature. "If you are so generous can you give me your bones?" asked the lord. Gada immediately tore open his body and pulled out his bones. From these the celestial artisans, the Ribhus, made Vishnu his mace. Gada's flesh turned into five metals — gold, silver, copper, iron and tin — which the Ribhus smelted for Vishnu's sword.

Vishnu once promised Shiva 1008 lotuses. To test his devotion, Shiva stole one of the lotuses. When Vishnu discovered this loss, he offered Shiva one of his lotus-shaped eyes instead. For this act, Shiva gave Vishnu a discus with jagged edge called the Sudarshan-*chakra* which rotates round the lord's finger. When flung, it beheads his enemies before returning to his hand.

Vishnu offering his eye in place of a lotus to Shiva

Musical Instruments

Every Hindu god is associated with musical instruments. Brahma has his lute, Shiva, his drum. Vishnu is associated with wind instruments like the flute, *bansuri,* or the conch, *sankha.*

Vishnu charms the innocent with his flute and warns the wicked with his conch. As Krishna, the lord played the flute in the pleasure-gardens of Vrindavana and blew the conch Panchajanya on the battlegrounds of Kurukshetra.

Divine beasts

When there is peace and harmony, Vishnu rests on the coils of the serpent Ananta-Sesha; when there is disorder, he rides the eagle Garuda to battle the forces of chaos and corruption.

Ananta-Sesha represents endless Time. When the world is dissolved, Vishnu — the lord of Time — rests on it; when the world evolves, the lord dances on its hood. Both Lakshmana and Balarama, brothers of Rama and Krishna respectively, are believed to be *avatar*s of Ananta-Sesha.

Garuda, the mighty eagle, the lord's mount and insignia, is said to be the sun itself, his golden wings being its rays, rising in the east and setting in the west guided by his master, Vishnu. Hanuman — Rama's monkey friend — is sometimes identified

Krishna playing the flute in Vrindavana; North Indian miniature painting

Vishnu and Lakshmi on Garuda;
North Indian painting

with Garuda. Vishnu is also associated with parrots, vehicle of the love-god. In fact Garuda, in paintings, is shown more as a beautiful parrot than a fierce eagle.

Sacred plants

Vishnu's spirit is said to reside in the banyan, *vata*, and the pipal, *ashvattha*, trees which are believed to be immortal and auspicious. In their shade he gave discourses when he incarnated as Kapila, Buddha, Datta and Narada. On their leaves he lies afloat when the waters of doom cover the surface of earth during *pralaya*.

The lotus in the lord's hand represents as well as detachment, for though this beautiful flower grows in muddy water, neither water nor dirt are ever seen sticking to its petals. Like the lotus, Vishnu is the partaker of life's pleasures who never gets ensnared by the charms of the world.

A cane of sugar, the shaft of the love-god's bow, is often used to represent Vishnu, Madana's father. Like the sweet sap of the sugarcane, life's *rasa* has to be squeezed out by anyone who truly seeks to enjoy the world.

Garuda supporting Vishnu and Lakshmi; Western Indian sculpture

Worship of Vishnu

There exists an extremely personal relationship between Vishnu and his devotees who look upon him as a friend, lover, parent, child, master or teacher and worship him accordingly.

Image

Beside any idol of Vishnu or his incarnations, is placed an idol of the lord's consort Lakshmi. She intervenes between Vishnu and his devotees like a mother approaching the father on behalf of her children.

The serpent Ananta-Sesha's hood serves as a parasol above them; in front of the shrine stands the Garuda-*dhvaja*, eagle-banner of the lord.

Shalagrama

The gods could not defeat the demon Shankhachuda because the chastity of his wife Vrinda protected him from harm. So Vishnu entered Vrinda's chamber taking the form of her husband, and the lady, unable to recognise the imposter, served him as a wife. As a result Vrinda unwittingly soiled her virtue and her demon-husband Shankhachuda, no longer protected by the power of her chastity, was killed by the gods.

When Vrinda discovered how Vishnu had tricked her, she cursed him to turn into the *shalagrama* stone.

The *shalagrama* stone is sometimes worshipped in place of Vishnu's idol.

Tulsi

Tulsi, a destitute woman, sometimes identified with Vrinda, was accused of infidelity and shunned by all. Finding no shelter in the three worlds she turned to Vishnu for help. But the gates of Vaikuntha were shut on her face. Lakshmi refused to let her in.

Tulsi stood in the courtyard of Vishnu's abode, under the open sky, helpless and humiliated. Her feet turned into roots, her arms sprouted leaves, and she turned into a delicate yet wild plant, her fragrance spreading all around.

The lord said, "By not abandoning her devotion to me, despite all odds, Tulsi has become my beloved, Vishnu-*priya*. She should be treated with dignity at all times — not as an unchaste woman, but as a venerable housewife, a *sumangali*."

Chapter XV

Shalagrama stones are found in the bed of the river Gandaki in Nepal and are characterised by spiral *chakra*-like markings.

A woman nurturing the *tulsi* plant

Image of Lakshmi-Narayana worshipped in household shrines; South Indian bronze idol

And so the *tulsi* plant is nurtured in the courtyard of every house, and is identified as Vishnu's Vrinda or Krishna's Radha, women whose devotion for the lord, though unrequited, never waned.

This sacred basil, *Ocymum sanctum*, is a fragrant, medicinal plant that keeps away mosquitoes and flies. No worship of Vishnu is complete without an offering of *tulsi* sprigs.

By convention, the *tulsi* leaf is not offered to Shiva, just as *bel* leaves which are dear to Shiva are not offered to Vishnu. *Tulsi* leaves are also not offered to images of the mother-goddess as the plant once annoyed Lakshmi by diverting Vishnu's attention during their lovesport.

Necklaces of tulsi beads are used as rosaries while chanting the name of the lord. These are kept in special cloth bags to prevent their contamination.

Sacred Symbols

Once, Savitri, the consort of Brahma, was late for a *yagna*. Vishnu created another woman called Gayatri to assist Brahma with the rituals. In anger Savitri cursed Vishnu, "Your footprints will be more venerable than your body." And so the footprints of Vishnu, Vishnu-*pada*, are considered very auspicious. They are drawn pointing towards the house, symbolising the arrival of divine grace.

Sacred symbols of Vishnu are often painted on the floor and the walls of the house to ensure his grace and to ward off malevolent spirits. These include Vishnu's conch and the discus, and sometimes the lotus, fish, lion, *makara*, turtle and *go-pada*, footprints of cows.

Another symbol associated with Vishnu, embodying the spirit of his consort Lakshmi, is the *swastika*, symbol of the benevolent sun and its rays. *Swastika* means *su asti*: let good things happen.

Sacred Marks

Vaishnavas identify themselves with a sacred mark called *urdhva-pundra* or *namam* painted on their forehead. Using sandalpaste or white clay, they draw two vertical lines that meet at the base. These lines represent Vishnu-*pada*, the foot-print of Vishnu, symbol of contemplation and reverence.

Between the lines is a red dot or a red line that represents Vishnu's active energy — his *shakti* — sometimes identified with his consort, Shree-Lakshmi.

Bedecked image of Ranchor-rai Krishna enshrined at Dwarka, Gujarat

Sacred days

Yogamaya is Vishnu's divine power, his *shakti*, embodied in a female form. Once when Vishnu was asleep on the cosmic serpent a demon called Muka caused havoc in the cosmos. Not wanting to disturb the lord's *yoga-nidra*, Yogamaya leapt out of Vishnu's body and killed the demon on *ekadashi* day. Pleased with her deed, Vishnu made Yogamaya the goddess of *ekadashi-tithi* and declared that whosoever worshipped him on that day would receive his grace.

On *ekadashi*, the eleventh day of the bright and dark halves of the lunar month, devotees chant the name of the lord, fast, visit temples, bathe in holy waters and perform charitable deeds.

Shrines

Vishnu shrines are established within great temple complexes or in households.

In his temples, Vishnu is treated as a god-king, with an army of temple staff — priests, musicians, dancers, cooks, cleaners, washermen, painters, artists — serving him. The temples are usually designed as Vaikunthas on earth with small shrines of other gods, godlings, consorts and celestial beings surrounding the main shrine of Vishnu.

In households, Vishnu is looked upon as the true master of the house, the family members being the tenants. His shrine occupies the central portion of the dwelling around which are located the living quarters, kitchen and storerooms.

Yogamaya, divine power of Vishnu, embodied in female form; South Indian bronze

Sacred Observances

To enhance the personal relationship between Vishnu and his devotee, certain practices are observed. These are:

Shravanam, or hearing about the lord. In gatherings people listen to sacred texts like the *Ramayana* or the *Bhagavatam* that retell tales of the lord's valour and grace. Lectures on *Bhagavad Gita* which contains the essence of Vaishnavism are also popular.

Vandanam, or praising the lord. In temple precincts people gather together and sing sacred songs, *bhajan*s and *kirtan*s, that describe the lord's attributes, his exploits and his benevolence. The hymns may be in Sanskrit, like the *Narayaniyam*, or in the vernacular, like the hymns of the Alvar saints compiled in the Tamil work known as *Nalayira-prabandham*.

Smaranam, or remembering the lord by chanting the 1008 names of the lord, or chanting one name of the lord 1008

A temple procession with Vishnu image; Mysore painting

The altar of Satya-Narayan *Mahapuja*

times. Some common chants, *japa*, are: 'Narayana-Narayana' or 'Hare Rama, Hare Rama, Rama-Rama, Hare-Hare; Hare Krishna, Hare Krishna, Krishna-Krishna, Hare-Hare,' or the more elaborate 'Om Namah Bhagavate Vasudevaya' which means 'salutations to the supreme lord of the cosmos'. People often greet each other with phrases like, "Hari Bol, "Jai Shri Krishna" or "Jai Shri Rama. These greetings make the lord an integral part of people's lives. It keeps away malevolent forces. It is said, one is forgiven for one's sins as many times as one utters the name of the lord.

Sevanam or serving the lord. The devotee treats the image of Vishnu as a real person, a divine guest. The image is roused from sleep, bathed with perfumed water, annointed with oil and sandalpaste, bedecked with flowers, silks and jewellery, invited for meals, fed non-spicy food cooked in pure butter, offered flavoured drinks and betel-nut, entertained with song and dance, saluted and petitioned before being put to bed with reverence.

Ceremonies in temples are far more elaborate than in household shrines. The priest, *pujari*, follows rules and guidelines laid down in the *Agama* texts. On special days, the idol is taken out in procession. Grand festivities are held on the lord's birthday and on days that commemorate his victories in battle.

Satya-Narayana *Mahapuja*

Householders and housewives worship god in a personal way that best expresses their devotion.

On special days, people invite priests to their homes or their place of work to perform the *Satya-Narayana Mahapuja*, the great ritual adoration of the supreme lord.

The image of the lord is placed on a pedestal decorated with flowers and leaves. *Tulsi* sprigs are offered to the lord as the 1008 names of Vishnu are chanted. The ritual can be performed only by married couples and is usually conducted to secure the lord's grace at the start of some important project or to thank the lord on its completion.

Ultimately, it is the emotion accompanying the ritual rather than the ritual itself that matters.

Vishnu being worshipped by a married couple; Modern calendar art

Festivals of Vishnu

Chapter XVI

Annual festivals are held in memory of the lord's many descents and triumphs.

Chaturmasa

Every year, Vishnu is said to rest on Ananta-Sesha through the four months of the rainy season. This period, known as *Chaturmasa*, is a time of social dormancy when journeys are not undertaken and marriages not solemnised. People stay at home and pray because the sun is on its inauspicious southern course, the *dakshinayana*, making nights longer and days colder.

The divine retreat begins on Shayani-*ekadashi*, the eleventh day of the waxing moon in the month of *Ashadha* (June-July), and ends four months later, on the eleventh day of the waxing moon in the month of *Kartika* (October-November), Prabodhini-*ekadashi*.

Tulsi-*vivaha*

When Vishnu rises after his four-month repose, he renews his pact of protecting the earth by ceremonially marrying the earth-goddess on the twelfth day of the waxing moon in the month of *Kartika*.

The goddess, represented by the *tulsi* plant, is wedded to the lord who is represented either by an idol or a *shalagrama* stone or a cane of sugar. This Tulsi-*vivaha* marks the beginning of the Hindu marriage season.

Vishnu sleeps through the four months of the rainy season, *Chaturmasa*

Tulsi plant is married to Vishnu, represented by a sugarcane, at the end of *Chaturmasa*

Dev-Diwali

Katrik-*poornima*, the full moon day that follows Tulsi's marriage is called Dev-Diwali to commemorate the day the lord descended upon earth as Matsya, the divine fish who saved the children of the earth — plants and animals — from the cosmic deluge.

Datta-*jayanti*

The full moon day of the month of *Margashisha* (December), marks the day Datta, the great *yogi* and *tantrik*, was born to the chaste Anasuya, wife of sage Atri. Datta embodies the spirit of Vishnu and is worshipped not as a god but as a divine teacher.

Makara-sankranti

December 22nd is the winter solstice, the shortest day of the year, after which the sun begins its northward journey, the *uttarayana*. Days gradually become longer and warmer. On January 14th each year, the sun-god Surya-Narayana rides his golden chariot into the house of Capricorn or *makara*, the abode of Madana, lord of love. It is an auspicious day known as Makara-*sankranti* and marks the winter harvest which is celebrated as *Lohri* in the north of India and *Pongal* in the south. Men fly kites and women distribute sweets.

Holi

This festival, held on the full moon day of *Phalguna* (February-March), marks the end of winter and the beginning of spring. It is a festival of love and joy, of colours and excitement, welcoming Madana, the lord of pleasure, who is the son of Lakshmi and Vishnu. It is a fun filled festival celebrated in anticipation of a joyful year ahead.

This festival, with sensual undercurrents, was the favourite of Radha and Krishna. Devotees who pour coloured water on their loved ones remember through song and dance the pranks of Krishna and the complaints of Radha.

On the eve of Holi great bonfires are lit to mark the death of the demoness Holika who got burnt herself when she tried to burn Prahlada, the devotee of Vishnu-Narasimha.

Rama-*navami*

Dashratha had three wives but no children. After numerous sacrifices, he became the father of four sons who embodied the spirit of Vishnu. The eldest, Rama, was a dutiful son, a loving husband and a noble king.

Krishna and Radha playing Holi; Pahari painting

He was born on *navami*, the ninth day of the bright half of the month of *Chaitra* (March-April). The day is marked by recitations of the epic *Ramayana* which recounts the story of Rama, the personification of virtue.

Akshaya-*tritiya*

On the third day of the bright half of *Vaishakha* (April-May) Renuka gave birth to Parashurama, the sixth incarnation of Vishnu. On this holy day, people buy gold, safe in the knowledge that the lord will protect their wealth from thieves just as he stopped the thousand-armed Kartaviryarjuna from stealing the cow Kamadhenu from the hermitage of sage Jamadagni.

Naga-panchami

On the fifth day of the waxing moon of *Shravana* (July-August), cobras are offered milk and worshipped as representatives of Ananta-Sesha, the cosmic serpent, keeper of the earth's fertility and destroyer of pests.

Narali Poornima

On the full moon night in the month of *Shravana* (July-August), fishermen throw coconuts in the sea, thanking the sea-god, Varuna, for holding aloft the bridge that enabled Rama to go to Lanka, the island kingdom of Ravana, to rescue his wife Sita. The day marks the gradual retreat of the monsoon winds which enables fishermen to return to the sea.

In some parts of India, oxen are worshipped to celebrate the birth of Balarama, Krishna's elder brother, lord of farmers.

Sisters tie sacred threads on the wrists of their brothers on this day and seek their eternal love and protection. This ceremony, called *Raksha bandhan*, was instituted by Sachi, the queen of the gods, who tied a thread round Vishnu's wrist seeking his support in the celestial battles against demons.

Radha said:

Ever since I saw Krishna
my eyes are drenched
in the waters of his love;
they keep filling with tears
they keep shedding the tears
they keep swimming and drowning
  in them
like pots of a water wheel
moving in and out of the well

—Bihari

Children dressed as Lakshmi and Narayana in a sacred enactment of Vishnu's lore during a Vaishnava festival

Krishna and his friends stealing butter; Painting from Orissa

Gokula-*ashtami*

This festival, commemorating the descent of Vishnu upon earth as Krishna, is one of the few to be celebrated in the dark half of the lunar month, on the eighth day of the waning moon of *Shravana*. Celebrations take place late at night. Images of the lord are placed in cradles and the tale of his descent as described in the *Shrimad Bhagavata Purana* is retold to delight his devotees.

The next day, as part of Nanda-*utsava*, youths come together and form human pyramids to get to pots of curds and butter tied high up in community squares, remembering Krishna who enjoyed raiding the dairies of Vrindavana.

Dussera

On Vijaya-*dashami*, or Dussera, the tenth day of the waxing moon of *Ashvina* (September-October) Rama triumphed over Ravana, the demon-king of Lanka who had abducted his wife. On the days leading up to Dussera the entire legend of Rama is relived on stage by drama-troops, especially in North India. This Rama-*leela* culminates with the burning of effigies of the demon Ravana, his brother Kumbhakarna, and his son Indrajit.

Effigy of Ravana burnt during Dussera

Diwali

Diwali or Deepavali, the festival of lights, is celebrated in the new moon night that comes after Dussera.

The day before Diwali is known as Naraka-*chaturdashi* when devotees celebrate the defeat of the demon Naraka at the hands of Krishna.

On the new moon night Lakshmi, Vishnu's consort, is worshipped by one and all. Lamps are lit and sacred diagrams are placed on the floors to welcome her. On this night, Vishnu helped Shiva defeat Parvati in a game of dice by manipulating the die using his power of delusion, *maya*. In memory of that event, people play dice during Diwali, a reminder that the final result of any deed rests in the hands of the lord.

The day after the new moon night is Bali-*pratipada* when Vishnu, as the dwarf Vamana, pushed Bali back into the netherworld. It is a day of festivities, when sweets are distributed.

Diwali also commemorates the return of Rama to Ayodhya after 14 years in the forest. Devotees express their joy by lighting lamps.

Crackers are also burst to mark the approaching end of *Chaturmasa* and to herald the return of Vishnu to drive away the demons.

Vishnu — the adorable child who was born on Gokula-*ashtami*; Tanjore painting

Rama's coronation;
Modern sculpture

105

Some Vaishnava shrines in India

Temples of Vishnu

There are 108 Vaishnava shrines located all over India. The following are some of the sacred sites of the lord:

Temples of Vishnu

Vishnu is enshrined in many parts of India in huge temple complexes surrounded by smaller shrines housing his consorts, his incarnations, his attendants and his devotees.

Temple of Badrinath located in Uttarakhand, Uttar Pradesh

Narayana of Badrika-puri

Located on the hills of Uttarakhand, Uttar Pradesh, the shrine of Badrinatha is considered by many to be the fountainhead of the Vaishnava religion. The site is named after the *badri* tree under which meditated Nara-Narayana, the lord's twin incarnations.

The idol of the deity, flanked by images of Nara-Narayana and Narada, is believed to have manifested itself from the sacred *shalagrama* rock. The present temple was rebuilt in the eighth century by the philosopher Shankaracharya.

Gadadhara of Gaya

Brahma wanted to perform a *yagna* in the holiest spot on earth. This happened to be in the living person of the *asura* Gaya who was so pious that anyone who saw him became immortal. So Vishnu pushed Gaya under the earth and held him down with his mace while Brahma performed the sacrifice upon Gaya's body.

The site where Gaya lies buried is located in Bihar and is marked by a shrine dedicated to **Gadadhara**, Vishnu-who-bears-a-mace. Nearby is a great temple enshrining Vishnu-*pada*, Vishnu's footprint, much revered by Vaishnavas.

In the yard of this temple grows the great banyan tree under which the Buddha is said to have meditated before going to Bodh Gaya where he attained enlightenment.

Tirupati of Venkatagiri

When Shree-Lakshmi disappeared from Vaikuntha after a disagreement with her lord, Vishnu descended upon earth looking for her. He found her in Kolhapur, Maharashtra, but she was too angry to return. So the lord decided to stay on earth until she had calmed down. He made the seven hills of Vyenkata, in Andhra Pradesh, his home because the hill-tops reminded him of the seven hoods of the serpent Ananta-Sesha.

Temple of Tirupati; Andhra Pradesh

Venkateshwara of Tirupati whose eyes are covered with his sacred mark

The eyes of the idol at Tirupati are so beautiful that they have to be covered with the *tilaka* otherwise his devotees would never leave the shrine and all worldly duties would be left unattended.

The lord married a local princess, the beautiful Padmavati, whose shrine is located nearby at Tiruchanur. Kubera, god of wealth, helped the lord meet his marriage expenses; Tirupati is still repaying the debt using money offered by his devotees. The wedding anniversary of the lord and his consort is celebrated each year during the *Brahmotsavam* festival.

Ranganatha of Srirangam

Vishnu as **Ranganatha**, lord of play, is seen resting on his serpent couch with his two consorts, Shreedevi and Bhoodevi , at his feet, at the vast temple complex of Srirangam, Tamil Nadu. This idol was given by lord Rama to Vibhishana, the pious brother of the demon Ravana, who unfortunately placed it on the ground before he reached his island kingdom of Lanka. As a result, the idol remained rooted to the spot, facing Lanka in the south instead of the traditional east.

This temple, where the eleventh century philosopher Ramanuja spent most of his life, houses a shrine dedicated to Andal, daughter of a temple priest, who refused to marry any mortal as she was in love with the lord himself. Also located here is the shrine of another great devotee of Ranganatha, Manavala Mamunigal, a Muslim princess.

Another Ranganatha temple is located at Srirangapatanam near Mysore, Karnataka.

Varadaraja of Kanchipuram

Brahma, the creator, performed a great fire-sacrifice at Kanchi, Tamil Nadu. Unfortunately he began the ritual without waiting for Saraswati, goddess of speech. Angered by this, the goddess turned herself into a fast-flowing river intending to wash away the sacrificial altar.

Ranganatha of Shrirangam, Tamil Nadu

Brahma appealed to Vishnu who immediately placed himself in the path of the river and diverted it, enabling Brahma's *yagna* to proceed uninterrupted. In gratitude Brahma installed the idol of Vishnu in this place naming him **Varadaraja**, the lord-who-bestows-boons.

Padmanabhaswami of Tiruvananthapuram

Tiruvananthapuram means the city of Ananta-Sesha, the celestial serpent. This city, the capital of Kerala, is built around the temple of **Padmanabhaswami**, whose 18 foot idol, the largest in India, can be seen reclining on the coils of the cosmic serpent in the dimly lit sanctum sanctorum. Devotees view the lord through three doors, one revealing his feet, another his navel from which rises the cosmic lotus, and one revealing his head and chest.

Temples of Vamana

Shrines of Vamana-Trivikrama are found within many temple complexes of south India. At Kanchipuram, Tamil Nadu, one can see the 35 foot idol of the divine dwarf Ulagalandar Perumal. Another small temple at Trikkakara near Cochin in Kerala marks the site where the demon-king Mahabali ruled the earth before being pushed into the netherworld.

Temple of Kurma

The only temple dedicated to the turtle incarnation of the lord is located at Srikurman in Andhra Pradesh. The deity consists of two stones, about two feet long, coming out of the ground. They represent the divine turtle's head and body. The temple faces east but Shri Kurma faces west, with his back to the entrance. A low caste devotee of the lord is said to have called out to him from the back of the temple with such devotion that the lord turned around to face him. Consequently the temple has two flag poles, one to the east and one to the west. The original temple was built about 2000 years ago, but it attained its present status after the Vedanta scholar Ramanuja rediscovered it on his way back south from Puri in the eleventh century A.D.

Varadaraja of Kanchipuram, Tamil Nadu

Shri Kurma, enshrined on the coast of Andhra Pradesh, near Vishakhapatanam

Temples of Krishna

The worship of Vishnu through the image of Krishna is extremely popular across India. Krishna, who is *leela purushottama*, playfulness personified, is the most delightful and humanised form of the divine lord.

Keshava of Mathura

Mathura, Uttar Pradesh, is the birthplace of Krishna. Within the temple here is a small room that looks like a prison cell where it is believed Krishna was born. Nearby is Rangabhoomi, the arena where Krishna killed his wicked uncle, Kamsa.

Temple of Ranchor-rai on the western coast of India at Dwarka, Gujarat

Gopala of Vraja

Krishna spent the first seven years of his life at Gokula and the rest of his childhood at Vrindavana. This sacred land standing on the fertile plains of Uttar Pradesh where the lord grazed his cows, played his flute, danced with *gopa*s and *gopi*s, is dotted with many shrines dedicated to Krishna, his beloved Radha, his foster father Nanda-*baba* and his elder brother Balarama-*dauji*. Many temples located here were demolished in the middle ages; the idols were taken to the houses of Rajput warlords in Rajasthan to protect them from marauders.

Dwarakadhish of Dwaraka

Dwaraka, the capital of Krishna's kingdom, is no more. It was destroyed by a great flood soon after Krishna left the earth. But the site is marked by two temples, one on the island of Bet-Dwaraka and a larger one on the mainland at modern Dwaraka on the coast of Gujarat. Here Krishna is worshipped as a king, **Dwarakadhish**. Nearby is the temple of his chief queen, Rukmini.

Vitthala of Pandharpur

While talking about his beloved Radha, Krishna's eyes filled with so much joy that it made Rukmini jealous. She ran out of Dwaraka and came to Pandharpur in Maharashtra. Krishna followed his queen to this village where lived Pundalik, one of Vishnu's greatest devotees. When the lord arrived at his devotee's house, he found Pundalik too busy taking care of his parents to attend to him. So the lord stood at the doorstep on a brick, *vit*, arms akimbo, waiting for Pundalik to finish his chores. The lord still stands there as Vitthalaswami, he-who-waits-for-his-devotee-standing-on-a-brick.

Vitthala and his consort Rakhumai or Rukmini, the presiding deity of Pandharpur, Maharashtra

This temple was the centre of the *Varkari-bhakti* movement, led by saints like Gyaneshvar, Tukaram and Eknath, that swept across Maharashtra in the middle ages.

Sreenathji, Vishnu who resides as
Krishna, beloved of mankind,
at Nathdwara, Rajasthan

Temple of Jagannatha at Puri, Orissa, where every year the presiding deity is taken on a chariot ride

Jagannatha of Puri

At Puri, Orissa, the lord Jagannatha-Krishna is worshipped along with his brother Balabhadra and his sister Subhadra. This holy spot attracted great *bhakta*s like Chaitanya Mahaprabhu and Shankardev and inspired the poet Jayadeva who wrote the classic *Geeta-Govinda* describing the love of Krishna and Radha.

After the mortal remains of Krishna had been cremated in Prabhas-Patan near Dwaraka, there rose from the ashes a great pipal tree that in time fell into the sea and made its way to the coast of Orissa where it was found by the local king, Indradyumna.

The king commissioned the celestial artisan, Vishvakarma, to carve out the image of the lord from the log of wood. Vishvakarma demanded complete isolation until the project was complete; but the impatient king broke his promise and entered the workshop before the idols were fully ready. And so, even today the idols have an unfinished look: flat faces, incomplete arms and no feet. The idols made of wood are replaced every twelve years.

The Jagannatha temple is associated with the great *ratha-yatra* that takes place on the second day of the waxing moon in the month of *Ashadha* (June-July) when the lord along with his brother and sister go to the shrine of their aunt, Gundicha, on colourful chariots made specially for the occasion.

Sreenathji of Nathdwara

This idol of the lord with arm upraised to greet his devotees was installed by Vajranabha, Krishna's great-grandson, at Vraja on the banks of the Yamuna. It was shifted to a *haveli* at Rajasthan in the seventeenth century to protect it from idol-breakers.

Idol of Chinna-Keshava installed at Udipi, Karnataka by Madhavacharya

This became the centre of *pushti marga* of the sixteenth century saint Vallabhacharya who sought union with the lord through joyful activities.

The temple owns many cows, one of which is supposed to have descended from the cows tended by Krishna himself at Gokula. Every day the lord is served opulent delicacies cooked in pure ghee.

It is said that Krishna once tore his garment while rushing back to the temple to greet his devotees. From that day on, it has been a custom to blow the conch announcing him several minutes before opening the altar doors.

Krishna of Guruvayoor

While Krishna was safe in the arms of his foster mother Yashoda in Gokula, his natural mother Devaki at Mathura missed him sorely. To console Devaki, the lord gave her an image of himself.

This image was given to Krishna's friend Uddhava before the destruction of Dwaraka. He gave the idol to Guru Brihaspati, preceptor of the gods, and Vayu, the lord of winds, who carried it to Guruvayoor in Kerala.

Keshava of Udipi

On the coast of Karnataka stands the temple enshrining the idol of **Chinna-Keshava**, the little Krishna. This idol was given to the 13th century philosopher Madhava by a sea-captain whose ship the saint saved from a storm by directing it to the shore.

It was made by Rohini, Krishna's step-mother, to please Rukmini, Krishna's chief consort, who had never seen Krishna as a child. After the destruction of Dwaraka, it was retrieved by Arjuna from under the sea.

The idol was installed facing the east but it turned west so that a low caste devotee Kanakadasa, who was prohibited from entering the shrine, could look upon him through a crack in the western wall.

Temples of Dattatreya

Dattatreya, an *avatar* of Vishnu, is worshipped not as a god but as a celestial teacher who through numerous temporal *Dattavatari gurus* expounded the true meaning of *yoga, tantra, jnana, bhakti and karma*. Temples dedicated to him are located in many parts of Maharashtra, Gujarat and Karnataka. Some are even found in Nepal, the legendary birthplace of Datta.

Idol of Krishna-Vishnu enshrined in Guruvayoor, Kerala

Krishna Temple at Udipi

113

Rama, Sita and Lakshmana of
Ayodhya

Temples of Rama

Various places associated with the legend of Rama,
Vishnu's most dignified and respected *avatar*, have
become places of pilgrimage. These include: Ayodhya,
Uttar Pradesh, where he was born and where he
reigned; Chitrakuta, Uttar Pradesh, where he refused
Bharata's offer to return to Ayodhya; Nashik,
Maharashtra, from where Sita was abducted by Ravana,
the king of *rakshasa*s; Kishikinda, Karnataka, where he
befriended Hanuman and the *vanar*s; Rameshvaram, Tamil
Nadu, where he propitiated Shiva and the sea-god,
Varuna, before building a bridge to Ravana's island
kingdom of Lanka.

Temples of the Buddha and Rishabha

Temples dedicated to the Buddha and Rishabha have been
built by Buddhists and Jains, though these communities
do not regard them as *avatar*s of Vishnu. One of the most
sacred shrines of the Buddha is located at Bodh Gaya in
Bihar where he attained enlightenment.

Temples of Parashurama

After killing unrighteous warriors and kings, Parashurama
hurled his blood-soaked axe into the western sea. The sea-
god Varuna recoiled in horror and drew back to reveal the
western coast of India which has ever since been
identified with the Bhargava warrior-priest.

Folk shrines dedicated to Parashurama and his mother
Renuka are found along the coast, especially around

Parashurama beheading Renuka;
Mysore painting

114

the border of Maharashtra and Karnataka. According to temple lore, Renuka was fascinated by the sight of a prince sporting with his wives on the banks of the river Narmada. This angered her husband, sage Jamadagni, on whose orders she was beheaded by Parashurama. Pleased with his son's unquestioning obedience, Jamadagni offered him a boon. "Bring my mother back to life," said Parashurama. Jamadagni immediately restored Renuka's head. Resurrected, she became a goddess, while her son became the guardian of her chastity.

Parashurama of Pedhe

In the eighteenth century, merchant ships of a Muslim princess were caught in a storm. The princess, who had heard tales of how Parashurama had controlled the sea with his axe, promised to build a temple dedicated to this warrior-priest if he saved her ships. The storm abated and the ships returned to the shore unharmed. In gratitude the princess built a temple to Parashurama at Pedhe, Maharashtra. The idol it enshrined was an ancient one found by local cowherds in a termite hill where a cow used to shed its milk. This idol of Parashurama is flanked by the images of Kala, lord of death and time, and Kama, lord of life and love.

Shri Parashurama of Pedhe, Maharashtra

Temples of Narasimha and Varaha

Vishnu as Varaha and Narasimha killed the demon-brothers Hiranyaksha and Hiranyakashipu. Composite images of these two incarnations are found in many parts of Andhra Pradesh.

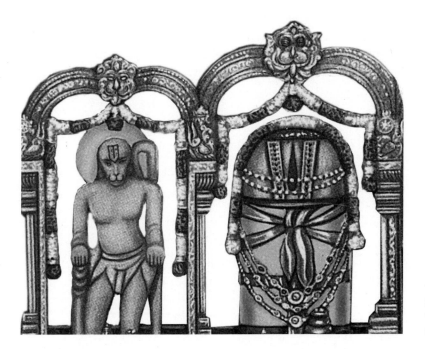

Varaha-Narasimha (left) of Simhachalam, Andhra Pradesh, is usually covered by a mound of sandalpaste (right)

115

Varaha-Narasimha of Simhachalam

The ferocity of this composite Varaha-Narasimha image installed by Prahlada himself is so great that it has the power to scorch the entire earth. So the idol is covered with sandalpaste throughout the year. The covering is removed and the idol is bathed only once in a year on Akshaya-*tritiya*, the third day of the waxing moon in the month of *Vaishaka* (April-May).

Nava Narasimha of Ahovalam

Nine images of the divine man-lion are located at this site associated with the killing of Hiranyakashipu. Here stands the *ugra-stambha*, the pillar of fury, from which the indignant lord emerged to save his devotee Prahlada from his wicked father. Nearby is the *rakta-kunda*, a lake where the lord washed his blood stained hands after killing the demon.

Narasimha, the man-lion incarnation of Vishnu, whose fury was restrained by his gentle consort, Lakshmi; Modern calendar print

Char-dham

It is said, Vishnu bathes at Rameshvaram, Tamil Nadu, dines at Puri, Orissa, holds court at Dwaraka, Gujarat and meditates at Badrika, Uttar Pradesh. These four holy-sites located in the four corners of India are the four sacred earthly abodes of the lord visited by his devotees.

Sapta-moksha-puri

Seven cities visited by Vaishnavas seeking salvation are: Ayodhya, the birthplace of Rama; Mathura, where Krishna was born; Ujjain, where Krishna was taught the scriptures by sage Sandipani; Dwaraka, where he reigned as king with Rukmini as his queen; Haridwar, Varanasi and Gaya, three holy cities where Vishnu's sacred footprint, Vishnu-*pada*, can be seen. Some even include the Southern city of Kanchi in this list because in this temple city the lord stands as the bestower of boons.

Vishnu-*pada*, Vishnu's holy feet;
Mithila floor pattern

Relevance of Vishnu, Today

For thousands of years, Vishnu has been part of the Indian heritage. He has been worshipped as the keeper of cosmic order, the preserver of life and the patron of worldly delight.

However, there are many who ask: what relevance does an ancient god like Vishnu have in modern times? Does he matter, here and now, in the age of automation and electronics?

Such questions arise from the belief that scientific discoveries and technological innovations have changed man.

They have not.

Man is still a bundle of fears and insecurities. He continues to be apprehensive about the future. And he is yet to answer that eternal question: what is the purpose of life?

Long ago, when death stared him in the face, King Parikshit asked the same question. In response, the sages narrated the sacred legend of Vishnu. As the tales unfolded, Parikshit found the answer he was looking for and died in peace. Like Parikshit, modern man can also find his answer in Vishnu.

Vishnu as the lord of righteous conduct; Stone idol from Cambodia

Keeping Faith

Vishnu's sacred legend begins with *pralaya*, cosmic dissolution, a time when chaos and evil overwhelm the cosmos. Vishnu leaps into this crisis as the fish **Matsya** and rescues Manu, father of mankind.

This legend is about surviving a crisis. Every man, at some time or the other, faces his personal *pralaya*: a

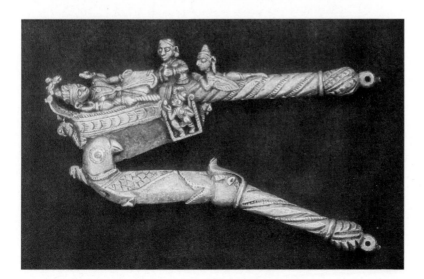

Vishnu reclining on the cosmic serpent; Bronze nutcracker from Maharashtra

O mind,
Worship the feet of Hari
When Prahlada grasped them
He became Indra,
When Dhruva sought refuge in them
He found paradise,
In the body of the dwarf
They measured the universe,
Their touch saved Ahalya,
They tamed Kaliya,
They supported Mount Govardhana,
When Krishna was cowherd
Mira is his servant —
The raft of unnavigable seas

— Meerabai

situation that threatens everything he believes in and all that he has built. It is a time when man needs faith: faith in himself, faith in the world. From faith springs hope, the determination to survive, the will to fight and triumph.

Matsya was a manifestation of Manu's faith. Holding on to it, Manu found refuge atop Mount Meru. Without faith, he too would have been swept away by the waters of doom.

Realising Dreams

Vishnu then turns into the turtle **Kurma**, and helps the *deva*s and the *asura*s churn wonderful things out of the ocean of milk.

The ocean of milk represents the infinite possibilities of existence. Man can churn whatever he wants out of his life, so long as he has aggressiveness tempered with discretion. But all effort is wasted if he lacks the patience and steadfastness of the turtle, the base of the celestial churn.

With the churning of the ocean, Shreedevi, goddess of wealth and fortune, comes into being. Though desired by all, she favours only Vishnu because only Vishnu possesses the qualities she appreciates — resourcefulness, tact, discipline and virtue.

Lakshmi, the beloved of Vishnu,
goddess of affluence and abundance;
Tanjore painting

118

Vishnu revealing his awe-inspiring
cosmic form; North Indian miniature
painting

Vishnu as the keeper of the cosmic cow; Modern calendar art

Vishnu as the dwarf priest Vamana; South Indian carving

Living Responsibly

Vishnu's other consort is the earth-goddess Bhoodevi whom he rescues from the bottom of the sea by taking the form of **Varaha**, the boar. Vishnu then becomes her eternal guardian, the blue sky, constantly watching over her well-being, ready to strike down anyone who abuses her.

As **Prithu**, Vishnu teaches man to treat the earth as a cow, to milk her resources without harming her. By describing earth as a cow, Vishnu drives home the point that the earth is a living entity that nourishes all life.

Sadly, modern man, in his scientific cynicism, refuses to believe in divine cows or divine cowherds. Disregarding the sacredness of rivers and forests, he has built industries that choke the earth and pollute the atmosphere. By doing so, he has aroused Vishnu's ire. Vishnu refuses to protect those who abuse his beloved Bhoodevi — and so the floods, the forest fire and the acid rain.

Accepting the Inevitable

Modern man sometimes behaves like Hiranyakashipu, the demon who believed he could outwit Nature and live forever. Hiranyakashipu secured a boon that would make it impossible for either an animal or a man to kill him. But Vishnu killed him anyway, by appearing as a being that is neither man nor beast, but both.

Man spends most of his resources trying to shield himself from emotional, social and financial problems. Yet problems manifest themselves, from the most unexpected quarters, in more ways than one. The legend of **Narasimha** is a reminder that no matter how hard one tries, one cannot escape the trials and tribulations of life. Man must therefore work towards fortifying himself in spirit against these turmoils.

Remaining Humble

Pride often blinds a man, makes him think he is immune to danger, makes him ignore minor issues until they turn into major ones and overwhelm him. This fact comes to light in the legend of **Vamana**, Vishnu's dwarf incarnation. The demon-king Bali, in his arrogance, did not perceive Vamana as a threat. Before he knew it, the dwarf turned into a giant and strode across the three worlds in three steps, crushing the demon-king underfoot.

Respecting Laws of Nature

There are laws in Nature; without them there would be chaos. There are rules in human society; without them there would be anarchy. These laws and rules, based on ethics and morality, maintain cosmic stability and social harmony. Vishnu institutes and maintains them.

When man breaks these rules, Vishnu tries to restore them: first by punishment, then by example. As **Parashurama**, he raises his axe and kills errant kings. As **Rama**, he upholds the law, sacrificing personal joy for the larger good of mankind, thus earning the reputation of being Vishnu's most venerable and august incarnation.

In the *Ramayana*, Rama stands out as a perfect man: a man who upholds righteousness even when faced with adversity, a trait often missing in the leaders and teachers of today.

Vishnu as the warrior-priest Parashurama; Rajasthani style miniature

Vishnu as the righteous Rama; Stone carving from Western India

121

Vishnu as Krishna with his beloved
Radha; Pahari miniature

Living Life to the Full

The legend of Rama focusses on the importance of
doing one's duty. But there is more to life than obeying
the law. Life is also about enjoying the beauty of the
cosmos. Vishnu highlights this fact by incarnating
as **Krishna**.

As Krishna, Vishnu balances delight with duty. As a child
he plays pranks on his mother. As a youth, he charms
the women of his village. He plays the flute and invites all
to dance around him in the meadows of Madhubana. But
then duty beckons. It is time to shoulder responsibilities,
go to Mathura and then on to Kurukshetra. It is time for
the music to stop.

In the *Mahabharata* epic, peopled with complex and
confused personalities, Krishna is the only one who has
a clear and balanced approach to life, a fact that comes
across in the *Bhagavad Gita*, his divine song.

For Vishnu, there is a time for everything — a time to
play, a time to work, a time to fight, and a time to give it
all up. There is a time to conform, a time to reform, a time
to rebel, a time to renounce. Similarly, for men there is
time to work and earn money, enjoy the pleasures of
worldly life, uphold traditions, perform duties. There is
also a time to retire, to sit quietly, contemplate and
meditate.

Vishnu as Krishna with his queen
Rukmini; Tanjore painting

Stepping Back and Taking a Look

In Vaishnava philosophy, the world is considered a playground, a *rangabhoomi*, and life a game, a *leela*. The rules make up *dharma*, the struggle to survive is *artha* and the fun within is *kama*.

This may sound frivolous. But the concept makes man aware that, like a game, life will one day come to an end. Before it ends, man must make sense of his presence in the playground.

To do this, man must play the game in the spirit of the game. Unfortunately, most of the time, man is so obsessed with winning that he forgets the rules of the *rangabhoomi*. In his delusion, *leela* becomes the end, not the means to realise the meaning of life.

To help man understand life, Vishnu insists on participation, for without first-hand experience one cannot discover the meaning behind the rules, the struggles, the pleasures and the pains.

Vishnu prescribes three modes of participation: *gyan marga*, participation with awareness, *bhakti marga*, participation with devotion and *karma marga* participation with detachment. These paths help man step back and witness the happenings of *rangabhoomi* and understand the true nature of *leela*. They lead to *moksha*, salvation, when winning and losing do not matter, when nothing binds man to the game and one is joyful even when it is time to leave the playground.

Vishnu as the sage Buddha who enlightened mankind; Stone carving

Vishnu flanked by an amorous nymph (left) who symbolises material pleasure and an austere sage (right) who symbolises spiritual bliss; Temple wall carving

123

Giving Value to Life

Vishnu's legend begins with *pralaya*; it also ends with *pralaya*, the dismantling of the universe by **Kalki**, Vishnu's final *avatar*.

In between is the cycle of life — universe's life, man's life. Vishnu is the protector, preserver and patron of this life. Though he is aware that all things are eventually washed away by the waters of doom, Vishnu strives to give life stability and order. And by doing so, he gives meaning and value to everything in this world.

Today, Vishnu's cosmic role as preserver, protector and patron of life has acquired immediate significance because the world seems to be decaying, degenerating, drifting towards destruction... the earth is being plundered, heritage is being ignored, culture is being eroded, all in the name of progress.

Everyone needs to find the spirit of Vishnu within themselves so that the earth is protected, heritage is preserved and culture, patronized. And by doing so, man can give value to his world and meaning to his life.

Vishnu as Kalki, the horseman of doom, who dismantles the corrupt world so that it can be reassembled in purity; Temple wall carving

124

Reaching for Excellence

When Vishnu was once asked how he could be recognised on earth, he replied, "I am **Vishnu**, the pervader; I exist everywhere, but I express myself best in all that is ideal, perfect, harmonious and beautiful:

"Amongst sacrifices, I am Yagna.
"Amongst chants, I am Omkar.
"Amongst mountains, I am Meru.
"Amongst elements, I am Jala.
"Amongst seasons, I am Vasanta.
"Amongst stars, I am Surya.
"Amongst rivers, I am Ganga.
"Amongst plants, I am Soma.
"Amongst trees, I am Ashvattha.
"Amongst flowers, I am Padma.
"Amongst snakes, I am Ananta-Sesha.
"Amongst turtles, I am Akupara.
"Amongst boars, I am Emusha.
"Amongst horses, I am Ucchaishrava.
"Amongst elephants, I am Airavata.
"Amongst swans, I am Hamsa.
"Amongst eagles, I am Garuda.
"Amongst bulls, I am Nandi.
"Amongst cows, I am Surabhi.
"Amongst lions, I am Narasimha.
"Amongst monkeys, I am Hanuman.
"Amongst gods, I am Indra.
"Amongst demons, I am Bali.
"Amongst damsels, I am Mohini.
"Amongst lovers, I am Madana.
"Amongst devotees, I am Narada.
"Amongst physicians, I am Dhanvantari.
"Amongst patriarchs, I am Prithu.
"Amongst kings, I am Mandhata.
"Amongst philosophers, I am Kapila.
"Amongst ascetics, I am Rishabha.
"Amongst poets, I am Valmiki.
"Amongst scholars, I am Vyasa.
"Amongst mystics, I am Datta.
"Amongst dwarfs, I am Vamana.
"Amongst avengers, I am Parashurama.
"Amongst relatives, I am Rama.
"Amongst farmers, I am Baladeva.
"Amongst cowherds, I am Vasudeva.
"Amongst teachers, I am Buddha.
"Amongst creators, I am Brahma.
"Amongst destroyers, I am Shiva.
"Amongst messiahs, I am Kalki."

To Vishnu does man offer the salute:

Om Namah Bhagavate Vasudevaya

ॐ नमः भगवते वासुदेवाय

125

108 Names of Vishnu

Devotees have tried to express Vishnu's divinity through 1008 names. Some of these names refer exclusively to particular incarnations. Others are shared with other divinities, like Shiva, for ultimately all gods are manifestations of the same godhead.

The following are 108 of the more popular ones:

Achyuta: restrained, unfallen; **Aditya**: sun; **Adhoksaja**: one who cannot be perceived by the senses; **Anantashayin**: he who sleeps on the serpent of eternity; **Aniruddha**: unrestrained; **Balaji**: eternal child; **Bhagavan**: complete manifestation of godhead; **Bhargava**: scion of the Bhargav clan (Parashurama); **Buddha**: enlightened teacher; **Chakrapani**: weilder of the discus, lord of life's cycle; **Chaturbhuja**: lord with four arms; **Chiranjeeva**: immortal; **Daityari**: killer of demons; **Damodara**: he whose stomach contains the whole cosmos; **Datta**: divine gift; **Dhananjaya**: winner of cosmic wealth; **Dharmadhikari**: keeper of world order; **Dhata**: support of all beings; **Ekatama**: single soul of the cosmos; **Gadadhara**: bearer of the mace; **Garudadhvaja**: he whose insignia is an eagle; **Ghanashyama**: dark as clouds (Krishna); **Gopala**: cowherd (Krishna); **Gopika-Vallabha**: lord of the cowgirls (Krishna); **Gopta**: hidden by viels of delusion; **Govinda**: protector of cows (Krishna) **Hari**: tawny; **Hayagriva**: horse-headed; **Hrishikesha**: lord of the senses; **Indravaraja**: Indra's brother; **Jagannatha**: lord of the world; **Jalashayin**: he who sleeps on water; **Janardhana**: beloved of the masses; **Ka**: the reason for all things; **Kaitabhajit**: killer of the demon Kaitabha; **Kalki**: the final saviour; **Kamalanayana**: lotus eyed; **Kanhaiya**: beloved of maidens (Krishna); **Keshava**: long haired; **Kiritin**: he who wears a crown; **Kshetragna**: lord of the field; **Krishna**: dark one; **Lakshmikanta**: lord of Lakshmi, goddess of wealth; **Lokanatha**: god of the people; **Madana-Mohana**: he who can charm Cupid; **Madhava**: husband of the mother-goddess; **Madhusudhana**: killer of the demon Madhu; **Manmatha**: pleasing the mind; **Manohara**: one who captivates the mind; **Mayin**: maker of illusions; **Medhavi**: wise and intelligent; **Mohana**: charmer; **Mukunda**: deliverer, liberator; **Muramardana**: he who killed the demon Mura; **Murlidhara**: flautist; **Narayana**: deliverer of mankind; **Naresh**: lord of man; **Narkantaka**: killer of the demon Naraka (Krishna); **Padmanabha**: one with a lotus rising from his navel; **Panchayudha**: bearer of five weapons; **Panduranga**: radiant lord; **Parmatma**: cosmic soul; **Parthasarathi**: charioteer of Partha-Arjuna, the Pandava (Krishna); **Patitapavana**: refuge of the helpless; **Pitambara**: one who wears yellow garments; **Pradyumna**: conqueror; **Prithu**: leveller; **Pundarikaksha**:

lotus-eyed; **Purna-purusha**: the primeval man; **Purushottama**: the ideal being; **Radhanatha**: lord of Radha (Krishna); **Raghava**: he who was a descendent of Raghu (Rama); **Raghuvamsi**: scion of the Raghu's dynasty (Rama); **Ramachandra**: as serene as the moon; **Ranganatha**: lord of colours; **Ranchor-Rai**: the king who avoided war (Krishna); **Rishabha**: bull amongst men; **Sankarshana**: plougher (Balarama); **Sharangin**: weilder of the bow, Saranga; **Shyam**: dark-one; **Shreedhara**: guardian of the goddess Shree; **Shreenatha**: lord of the goddess Shree; **Shreenivasa**: he who lives with Shree; **Shreevastava**: on whose chest resides fortune; **Subhanga**: he with a alluring body; **Svabhu**: he who created himself; **Tirupati**: lord of goddess Shree i.e. Tiru; **Trivikrama**: he who covered the cosmos with three steps (Vamana); **Upendra**: younger brother of Indra; **Urugaya**: one whose gait is wide (Vamana); **Urukrama**: one with vast strides (Vamana); **Vasudeva**: lord of elements; **Vaikuntha**: lord of cohesion; **Vallabha**: beloved husband; **Vamana**: dwarf; **Vanamali**: he who wears garlands of wild flowers; **Varadaraja**: the king who bestows boons; **Varaha**: the boar who raised earth from the ocean floor; **Vatapatrashayin**: Vishnu resting on the banyan leaf floating on the waters of doom; **Venkateshvara**: god of the hills; **Vidhu**: expert; **Virata-purusha**: the cosmic being; **Vishnu**: all pervader; **Visvaksena**: the defence of the cosmos; **Visvarupa**: one with a cosmic form; **Vitthala**: lord who stands on a brick; **Vyasa**: compiler of knowledge; **Yagna-purusha**: lord of the sacred rite.

Vishnu sleeping on Ananta-Sesha, the serpent of eternity (background) and standing between his consorts Bhoodevi, goddess of earth, and Shreedevi, goddess of fortune (foreground); relief from Shrirangam temple, Tamil Nadu

Glossary

adi	:	primal
amrita	:	nectar of immortality
apsara	:	damsel
artha	:	economics
ashwamedha	:	power of the horse
asura	:	demon of darkness
avatar	:	incarnation; descent
bel	:	plant sacred to Shiva; wood apple
bhakta	:	devotee
bhakti	:	devotion
bhukti	:	pleasure
bhoo	:	earth
brahmacharya	:	student-life; continence
brahmana	:	priest
chakra	:	wheel; disc
dampati	:	married couple
dasha	:	ten
deva	:	lords of light
dhvaja	:	flag
doota	:	messenger, angel
dharma	:	sacred laws sustaining the cosmos; duty
gada	:	mace; club
garbha	:	womb
go	:	bovine
gopa	:	cowherd
gopi	:	milkmaid
gow	:	cow
grihastha	:	conjugal-life
guru	:	teacher
jnana	:	knowledge
jala	:	water
kalpa	:	aeon
kama	:	pleasure
kamandalu	:	water-pot
karma	:	action that leads to reaction
kshatriya	:	warrior
kumar	:	boy
leela	:	game
loka	:	realm
maithuna	:	sexual union
manthan	:	churning
maya	:	illusion; mirage
moksha	:	salvation
naga	:	Cobra serpents
namah	:	salutations

nidra	:	sleep
om	:	mystical sound
padma	:	lotus
patala	:	netherworld
prakriti	:	universal substance; Nature
pralaya	:	cosmic dissolution
puja	:	worship; ritualistic adoration
purusha	:	man; cosmic spirit
rakshasa	:	demon
rangabhoomi	:	arena; stage
rasa	:	vitalising fluid
rati	:	erotic pleasure
rishi	:	seer; sage
samsara	:	mundane world where things constantly change
samskara	:	rites of passage
samudra	:	ocean
sankha	:	conch-shell
sanyasa	:	renunciation
sapta	:	seven
shakti	:	power
shalagrama	:	sacred Vaishnava stone
shree	:	wealth and splendour
shudra	:	serf
sumangali	:	lucky woman
Suvarnabhoomi	:	golden land; Burma; Thailand, Cambodia
Suvarnadvipa	:	golden island; Indonesia
Swarga	:	heaven
tantra	:	occult; ritualistic mysticism
tantrik	:	practitioner of the occult
tapas	:	austerity; penance
tulsi	:	plant sacred to Vishnu; basil
tirthankara	:	bridge builder
vahana	:	mount
vairagya	:	renunciation
vaishya	:	merchant
vanaprastha	:	retirement; forest-dwelling
vibhuti	:	emanation
vidya	:	knowledge
vilasa	:	pleasure
vrata	:	sacred observance or vow
yagna	:	fire-sacrifice
yaksha	:	gnome; goblin; forest spirit
yoga	:	mysticism through mental discipline
yuga	:	era

Vaikuntha with Vishnu resting on Ananta-Sesha surrounded by his wife, his soldiers, his companions and his angels, the Vishnu-*dootas*; Temple wall carving from Deogarh

Select Bibliography

Origins and Development of Vaishnavism:
Suvira Jaiswal

Mahabharat: Kesari Mohan Ganguli

Shrimad Bhagvatam: Kamala Subramaniam

Valmiki Ramayan: Makhan Lal Sen

Krishna: Pavan K. Varma

Hindu Myths: Wendy D. O'Flaherty

Hindu Mythology: W.J. Wilkins

Vishnu and his incarnations: Shakti Gupta

Bhagvad Gita: Swami Chinmayananda

Holy places and temples of India: John Howley,
Jada Bharata Dasa

Metamorphosis of Indian Gods: Marta Jakimowicz-Shah

Wonder that was India: A.L. Basham

Vaishnavism, Shaivism and Other Minor Religions:
R. G. Bhandarkar

Myth and Reality: D.D. Kosambi

Indian Mythology: Veronica Ions

Note: Vaishnava lore retold in this book has been taken from *Vishnu Purana, Bhagavata Purana, Narada Purana, Garuda Purana, Padma Purana, Kurma Purana* as well as the *Ramayana, Mahabharata* and *Harivamsa*. Some plots, like the filial relationship of Vishnu and Indra, have been gleaned from the *Veda*s while others, like the beheading of Vishnu, from the *Brahmana*s and the *Devibhagavata Purana*. Most tales, especially temple lore, exist only in oral tradition and have no textual references.